Arto der Haroutunian is Armenian and was born in Aleppo, Syria. In the early fifties his father, who was a priest of the Armenian Apostolic Church, was invited to head the local church in Manchester and brought the family over to settle in England. Arto der Haroutunian qualified at Manchester University as an architect and set up his own practice.

In 1970, with his brother, they set up their first Armenian restaurant specializing in authentic Middle Eastern dishes. He has always been interested in good food and was fortunate enough to have an excellent teacher – his mother, whose advice and guidance was always sought over the preparing of menus for the restaurants.

Apart from catering and architecture, his main interest is painting, with which he has achieved a considerable degree of success. He has exhibited all over the world with works in many major collections. He is married with a young son.

... for Magometians in ... Armenia, and was born in
Aleppo, Syria. In the early sixties his father, who was a
priest of the Armenian Apostolic Church, was invited to
teach and ... trade in Manchester, and although he
mainly over ... abortive in England. After the ... he trained
qualified at Manchester University as an architect and set
up his own practice.

In 19.. while his brother ... they set up Harvey Courtney ...
an restaurant specialising in authentic Middle East ...
dishes. He has always been interested in good food and
was fortunate enough to have an excellent teacher — his
mother, whose recipes and guidance was always sought
over the preparing of dishes for the restaurant.

Apart from cooking and architecture, his main interest
is painting with which he has achieved a considerable
degree of success. He has exhibited all over the world
with works in many public collections. He himself ... still
a young self ...

ARTO DER HAROUTUNIAN

Modern Jewish Cookery

Recipes from Israel

PANTHER
Granada Publishing

Panther Books
Granada Publishing Ltd
8 Grafton Street, London W1X 3LA

Published by Panther Books 1985

ISBN 0-586-06168-1

Printed and bound in Great Britain by
Collins, Glasgow

Set in Times

Contents

Acknowledgement

My grateful thanks to all the authors and publishers from whose works I have quoted. If, unwittingly, some have not been mentioned – my deepest apologies.

Anecdotes and poetry have, where necessary, been translated and edited from the original by the author.

Note: All recipes serve 6 people unless otherwise stated.

Introduction

'We have been the chosen people long enough; God should now choose another one.' *In King David's Footsteps*, Hans Habe

History and People

As a political expression, Israel came into being with the declaration of its own independence on 14 May 1948. It was recognized almost immediately by the United States of America, the Soviet Union and Britain (1949).

The Proclamation of Independence was read in the Art Museum of Tel Aviv to a Council of Jewish leaders in Palestine by David Ben Gurion, the provisional Head of Government, and thus, after nearly two thousand years of wanderings, the children of 'Biblical Israel' re-created their historic homeland.

Who were these 'children of Biblical Israel'?

Abraham (the historic founder of the Israelites) lived about 1850–1800 B.C. He hailed from Ur of the Chaldees (Southern Iraq) and was the head man of a small tent-dwelling tribe (very much like the nomadic Bedouins of Arabia today).

Abraham never settled down nor did his children; nearly a thousand years later, after the conquest of Canaan, they still preferred to live in tents. Thus they roamed all over the region. Some such as Jacob went to Mesopotamia, others like Joseph and his brothers settled in Egypt where the rich, fertile land was ideal for cattle-raising, especially in times of famine.

About four hundred years later, under the leadership of Moses, the Israelites escaped from Egypt, accompanied

by a 'mixed multitude'.[1] Moses[2] was allegedly born an
Israelite but was adopted by Pharaoh's daughter and
received the highest forms of education of his day. He had
great sympathy for the poor, downtrodden shepherds and
slaves on forced labour, had killed an Egyptian foreman
and escaped to Sinai. He worked as a shepherd for Jethro[3]
and married his daughter.

While in Sinai, Moses retired to one of the mountain
peaks to meditate and received a divine revelation. As a
result he recorded the Ten Commandments on tablets of
stone. Later an Ark was made in which the tablets were
deposited and which was carried with the people when
they moved camp.

Under the leadership of Moses, the Israelites returned
to Palestine, (though not before extensive tribal reorgani-
zations were undertaken in the Sinai peninsula).

For forty years they wandered the deserts gradually
moving northwards, infiltrating Palestine, where the Israelites found themselves amongst 'Canaanites, Hittites,
Amorites, Perizzites, Hivites and Jebusites. They married
the daughters of these peoples and gave their own daughters in marriage to their sons and served their gods.'
(Judges iii, 5)

Thus the Israelites amalgamated with the people of the
land. Meanwhile on the coastal plain another people,
called the Philistines and who were sea-borne invaders of
Greek origin, had established themselves. They were
industrially more advanced than the Israelites and much
more numerous. Having mastered the southern coastal
plain they began to penetrate the plain of Esdraelon and
by the middle of the eleventh century B.C. they were
forcing their way up into the mountains (the lands settled
by the Israelites).

Inevitably there followed battles, wars and massacres.
In this crisis the prophet Samuel rose to fame. He was
asked by the elders of his day to name a King to lead

them. He anointed Saul who defeated the Ammonites, and then the Philistines at Gaba (five miles north of Jerusalem). Saul also defeated the Amalekites, killing every human being regardless of age or sex, upon Samuel's instruction – but unfortunately for him he had not carried out the latter's orders to the letter. Samuel denounced his disobedience and anointed David as a rival king.

Under King David (1000–961 B.C.) Jerusalem was conquered and turned into the capital of the Kingdom, to complete the territorial union between the northern and southern tribes. David also made it the religious capital when he brought the Ark up to Jerusalem. Having consolidated his hold and his position David embarked on campaigns of conquest. He encouraged the inhabitants of the captive lands to integrate with the Israelites – indeed David was a great believer in integration. Bathsheba, whom he married (after having arranged the death of her husband Uriah), was a Hittite and David's own grandmother had been a Moabitess.

The reign of David was for Israel the military stage in her life history and as with most nations, the military phase was followed by the commercial and aesthetic age of David's equally famed son Solomon (961–922 B.C.), who was instinctively a man of peace, more interested in construction and administration. It was he who built the first temple, in 950 B.C., surrounded with a large quarter centred about the royal Palace where he held court in great splendour. He used unpaid labour 'from all Israel'. Yet due mainly to his extravagance towards the end of his reign he lost the goodwill of his subjects (he was obliged to sell twenty towns on his northern border to the King of Tyre). He died about 927 B.C. After Solomon's death the monarchy split into two parts, Judah and Israel.

Internally unstable, with dynasties changing frequently, the Kingdom of Israel came under heavy pressure from outside until all these endless, petty rivalries were over-

shadowed by the might of Assyria and Shalmaneser V
(727–722) finally crushed what was left of Israel and thus
after two hundred years the northern kingdom ceased to
exist. The population was deported (more than 20,000),
some to northern Iraq, others to Iran where they disappeared among the local inhabitants. They were replaced
by the importation of a new, mixed population, (a device
often used by great powers to 'scramble' all the population
of their empires).

Judah was more fortunate; it survived for another 135
years (largely through an alliance that King Hezekiah
struck with Egypt and Ethiopia). But here, too, gradually,
there grew corruption, religious laxity, the rich oppressing
the poor; 'the free democracy of tribal and desert tradition
had gone. Judah, moreover, suffered from one delusion
which had not affected Israel. The royalist political propaganda had disseminated two ideas; firstly that Jerusalem
was the residence of Yehwah and would never be conquered; secondly, that the house of David would rule for
ever'.[4]

In 598 B.C. Nebuchadnezzar with his mighty Babylonians arrived and Jerusalem surrendered. The King
(Jehoiakim) and the leading citizens as well as part of the
population were carried off to Babylon. As though this
was certainly not enough, ten years later the Babylonians
returned and completely destroyed Judea, Jerusalem
being razed to the ground. Solomon's temple was plun-
dered and then destroyed. Many Judeans escaped to
Egypt, Syria, Ammon and Moab.

> How doth the city sit solitary, that was full of people!
> how is she become as a widow! she that was great among
> the nations, and princess among the provinces,
> how is she become tributary! . . .
> Judah is gone into captivity because of affliction . . . she
> dwelleth among the heathen, she findeth no rest.
>   Lamentations of Jeremiah, Chap. I

The Jewish Diaspora may be said to have begun in Babylon and still continues to date. It was in Babylon that the Mosaic Law (Torah) took on its final form and many great works of teaching and devotion were written. The Pentateuch was re-edited, Leviticus being inserted to record the ritual of the ruined Temple. A different type of religious assembly evolved for the first time; prayers and devotion replaced ritual and sacrifice. These developments assured the Jewish people's survival.

Babylon made way for Cyrus of Persia who believed in religious tolerance. Jews were allowed to return to Palestine. Most refused to go, but about 42,000 elected to return. The temple was reconstructed under the leadership of Nehemiah and Ezra (the scribe) in 520 B.C.

Ezra was a remarkable man who helped to change the history of Judea. He was an outstanding reformer and his principal act of reform was the prohibition of marriage between Jews and the rest of humanity. 'The holy race was henceforth to be isolated from Mankind . . . the prohibition of intermarriage was an entirely new idea. The Israelites had been freely intermarrying with the people of the land for 800 years . . . Ezra shows the same confusion between "race" and religion as still befogs Jewry.'[5]

In 333 B.C. the Persian Empire collapsed under the advance of Alexander of Macedon and, although the conquerors left the Jews alone to continue their way of life, the Hellenistic period was responsible for further Jewish emigration.

After the death of Alexander his empire fell apart and after many wars was divided into two: the Seleucid and the Ptolemid. The leaders of these empires tried to persuade Greeks to emigrate to Syria and Egypt. Greek businessmen and ordinary settlers poured into the Middle East, building cities and settlements. To these towns too came Jews.[6]

The influx of Greeks changed the ethnic composition of

Syria, Lebanon and the coastal plain of Palestine down to
our times. 'Meanwhile the Hellenization of Jerusalem had
been started by the Jews themselves. This was no treason
against Judaism, the Greeks were the leading nation as
the US was after the Second World War. To imitate them
was modern; not to do so was old-fashioned.'[7]

In 200 B.C. Antiochus III captured Palestine and evicted
the Ptolemies. Antiochus IV occupied Jerusalem, dese-
crated the temple and the Jewish religion was prohibited.
The answer to these persecutions was the Maccabean
revolt (167 B.C.). A priest, Mathathiah of Hasmon, killed
a government official, then with his five sons took to the
hills, whence he raided villages, killing Hellenized Jews
and Greeks. After his death his son, Judas Maccabeus,
assumed command. Meanwhile Syria granted Judea (now
under Maccabean rule) a measure of political autonomy.
The state expanded until 63 B.C. when the new power
(Rome) under Pompeii captured Jerusalem.

The Roman occupation of Palestine marked the beginning of a long period of control which was not lifted until
after 1948. Palestine was declared a Roman Protectorate
which was ruled by the 'House of Herod'.

Herod, the son of Antipater, ruled Judea against many
difficulties. The Judeans hated him for co-operating with
Rome. Rome in turn was suspicious of his attempts at
neutrality since his domain was of vital importance to
Rome. (It was half-way between Syria and Egypt, two of
the most wealthy provinces of the empire.)

Herod built a new Temple as well as many public
buildings in Jerusalem. He rebuilt Samaria (Caesarea
which subsequently became the capital of Roman
Palestine). He also built the desert retreat of Masada near
the Dead Sea.

After Herod's death (at the age of seventy) his land was
divided into three: (a) Judea went to his son Archelaus
who ruled so badly that he was exiled to Gaul in 6 A.D. (b)

Herod Antipas was given Galilee and Peraea; (c) Philip received Gaulonitus and Trachonitis. Philip died heirless and his lands were incorporated in the Roman province of Syria, while Herod Antipas (the man who beheaded John the Baptist) was finally exiled to Gaul for intrigue.

The Herodians were appointed and dismissed at the whims of the Roman emperors. Conditions too in Judea were deteriorating. There were uprisings and riots and the nationalists were now out of hand. They seized Masada and massacred the garrison. All over the land Jews and Gentiles murdered senselessly; the 12th Roman Legion was decimated and, in short, Palestine was in chaos. 'Many of the most eminent Jews' left Jerusalem quietly, while the rebels set up a government under the leadership of Ananus with Ben Gurion as his deputy, but Jerusalem was in anarchy; 'those who were desirous of war, by their youth and boldness were too hard on the aged and the prudent men . . . they got together to rob the people of the country in so much that for barbarity and iniquity those of the same nation did in no way differ from the Romans'.[8]

Early in 68 A.D. Roman columns cleared the country east of Jordan, but their leader, Vespasian, was declared emperor. He therefore halted his expedition and sailed back to Rome. His son, Titus, took Jerusalem in September of 70 A.D. However, Jewish nationalism did not die and in 115 A.D. as well as 132 A.D. rebellions once more broke out all over Palestine.[9]

Under later Roman emperors the Jews remained quiet and were ruled almost autonomously by the patriarchs of the House of Hillel. These were times of vital spiritual developments; the Mishna was codified, the Palestinian Talmus was composed – two works which have influenced Jewish life for two thousand years.

The advent of Christianity, its growth, development and final dominance of the political and social infrastruc-

ture of the world from the first century until the advent of
Islam (seventh century) was perhaps – with only two other
exceptions, the Spanish Inquisition and the Nazi holocaust
– the most tragic period of Jewish history.

For several decades after the crucifixion the Christians
remained a small Jewish sect and were regarded as
heretics. They were stoned to death, crucified; Herod
Antipas 'laid violent hands on some who belonged to the
church. He killed James, the brother of John with the
sword and when he saw that it pleased the Jews, he
proceeded to arrest Peter also' (Acts 12, 1 and 2).

It befell Paul to change Christianity from a sect of
Judaism to a separate religion. He simplified the religion,
rejected the Jewish dietary laws and the rite of circumci-
sion, putting the emphasis on to faith in Christ.

The antagonism increased. About 90 A.D. the Jewish
Patriarch 'ordered the daily cursing of Christ in the
synagogue'. The Christians, after the expulsion from the
synagogue, lost their Jewish privileges and were actively
persecuted in Judea. 'But probably the principal cause of
hatred between Jews and Christians was competition in
the mission fields. It is rarely appreciated nowadays that,
before Christianity, the Jews were a powerful community
which was rapidly converting the Roman world. They
were understandably indignant when the Christians whom
they considered to be Jewish renegades, entered into
competition with them in converting pagans.'[10]

Until the fourth century Jews and Christians were
minorities in the pagan Roman Empire, but after the
conversion of Constantine (306–337) the Christians took
over and intolerance of both Jews and pagans increased.

The Visigoths in Spain persecuted their Jews, otherwise
– whether in Byzantium or in Persia – Jews were tolerated; they lived and prospered and indeed a 'Jewish'
kingdom was even established in Yemen from 200–236
A.D., when a local King was so impressed by Jewish

monotheism that he forcibly converted his entire court to the new religion.

At the beginning of the seventh century a new religion, 'Islam', led by the prophet of Allah – Mohammed – swept over the dunes and deserts of Arabia and in a short period of some 100 years (637–732), created the greatest empire ever known, stretching from the shores of the Atlantic to the Indian Ocean and the borders of China.

The rise of Islam signalled the death of Christianity, since its wealth had vanished, the trade routes were closed, the cities had shrunk, universities were closed and Europe became an agricultural continent.

The blockage of Europe by the Arabs opened an era of prosperity for the Jews, for Judaism was the 'cousin' of both religions. The Jews were half-brothers to the Arabs; they were not involved in the wars, but acted as middle men and they alone could live, travel and prosper in Christian and Muslim states.

Thus Jews flocked into Muslim Spain, Damascus and Baghdad and were the ancestors of the Sephardim of today. Jews in Spain were called to high posts. Hasdai Ibn Shaprut was a minister in the court of Abd-el-Rahman III; Moses Ibn Mainon, Abraham ben Ezra and Benjamin of Tudela who wrote *Itinerary of Benjamin of Tudela*, an excellent source on the twelfth century, were all Jews.

In Europe however, though tolerated, Jews were prone to attack, insult and envy – they were far better educated than their neighbours. There was no Christian university in Germany for example until the middle of the fourteenth century but the Rhinelands had what were practically Jewish universities in the era of the First Crusade (1096).[11]

The poverty, the suffering of the people, the 'Black Death', false accusations and falser rumours spread discord and hatred which were deliberately channelled against the 'Muslim lovers', ie Jews, and the whole charade (corrupted by political and economic misadventures) culminated in the Crusades which lasted 100 years and brought more sufferings, devastations and intolerance (the repercussions of which are still felt today, eg the problems of Lebanon, Cilicia (1920–30) and the Arab-Israeli conflicts).

The Jews, scattered as they were all over the then known world, fared according to the political conditions of their native region. Thus they lived in safety and substantial prosperity in Arab Spain from 712–1492, in Poland 900–1590, the Ottoman Empire 1492–1920, and England from 1655 onwards.

For a time they even had another 'Jewish Kingdom', that of the Khazars who were a Mongoloid people from central Asia and whose leader in about 740 adopted Judaism. This Jewish Kingdom was short-lived and in about 900 A.D. the Khazars were overrun by new Mongolian tribes from the East. The Jews, ie people of Jewish faith, were scattered all over Russia, the Ukraine and Poland.[12]

Jews were welcomed in Poland by Casimir III (1337–1370), but during the counter-reformation a great number of them moved to the Ottoman Empire, where at that period there was tolerance; while Jews were persecuted in France and Spain[13], they were well looked after by the rulers of the new Eastern Empire: 'A map of Jewish migration would offer an outline of Jewish experience. Jews moved like a river, seeking out the areas of least resistance. Tolerance brought an influx, persecution an exodus.'[14]

Throughout the centuries people of 'Jewish' faith kept to themselves. Jewish communities passed their own ordinances; most Jewries possessed judical powers over Jews and could sentence them to fines or death.

A Jewish community often owned an inn and a hall for festive occasions. Jews were better dressed, better housed and far better educated than their Christian counterparts. They were also home-loving and caring – 'Jewish men spent their leisure at home among relatives to avoid ritual impurity and, as a result, were above the average standards of sexual morality in their countries of residence.'[15]

The middle of the eighteenth century produced the first breath of liberalism in Europe which also affected Jewish thoughts. As liberalism spread, more and more privileges were accorded to minorities, including Jews, throughout Europe.[16]

'Jewish influence in the Christian world reached its climax in the first quarter of the twentieth century . . . meanwhile Jewish nationalists began to express the fear that if the Jews as a whole mingled with the Gentiles and became assimilated with them, the entire community would eventually lose the Jewish individuality which it had hitherto preserved by segregation . . . they began, therefore, to dream of establishing a territorial centre for the Jews and so transforming Jewry into a community kept together by nationalism.' Thus said Nevill Barbour on what has become a major Jewish theme, 'Zionism', or rather the evolution of Zionism, the germs of which were seeded thousands of years before as the zealots fought to the death on the fortress rocks of Masada.

The great 'dreamer' of Jewish nationalism was Theodor Herzl (1860–1904) who in 1897 in Basle, Switzerland wrote 'In Basle I established a Jewish state. If I were to say that aloud today, universal laughter would be the response. Maybe in five years, certainly in fifty years, everybody will recognize it.'

The man who more than any other transformed Herzl's Zionist dreams into action was Chaim Weizman, who laboured tirelessly for the Zionist cause. In 1917 the famed Balfour Declaration was issued, wherein it was stated that 'His Majesty's Government view with favour the establishment in Palestine of a national home for the Jewish people.'

In successive waves of immigration Jews made their way to Palestine, to settle and cultivate land purchased by the 'Jewish National Fund'.[17]

In 1909 the first Jewish city for 2000 years was founded – Tel Aviv, on the outskirts of Haifa. In the same year the first kibbutz, Daganya, was established.

The Balfour Declaration was published six weeks before the Turks surrendered to General Allenby. The League of Nations later made special reference to it in entrusting Great Britain with the mandate for Palestine; the mandate seemed for a time as if it might succeed. After large influxes in 1924, 1925 and 1926 the figures petered out in 1927 and 1928. Then the Nazis came to power in Germany and the persecution of the Jews began, culminating in the gas chambers of Auschwitz and the death of 6 million people.

The structure of the mandatory government followed the familiar British colonial pattern with a high commissioner exercising wide authority and assisted by a small, all-British executive council of senior officials. Britain attempted little economic advancement. The country was mapped; bridges, roads and railway communications were developed. The ports of Haifa, Acre and Jaffa were also improved.

In 1937 a Royal Commission under Lord Peel advocated partition. The Arabs objected, arguing that such action would only perpetuate a Zionist entity in Palestine. The Woodhead Commission allocated an even smaller area to the Jews which was immediately rejected by the Zionists.

By now the war had broken out in Europe and the persecution of Jews commenced in earnest. Those who were able to escape the gas chambers were unable to reach the only safe haven – Palestine. Illegal refugees from Europe were deported to Cyprus, Mauritius and, in some cases, even back to Europe. This policy (in view of the extreme Nazi atrocities being perpetuated against the Jews), led to extremist Zionist terrorism in Palestine.[18]

After the war anti-British feeling was very strong. In 1945–6 Britain and the USA proposed a new plan for partition. This too was immediately rejected by the Arabs and the Jews.

In 1947 Britain referred the whole question to the United Nations, and its special Committee on Palestine recommended that the mandate should end and the country be divided into Jewish and Arab regions. In this arrangement the Arab state was to include the central and eastern area (encompassing Nablus, Jerusalem, Bethlehem and Hebron as well as the strip of Mediterranean coast from Gaza to the Egyptian border), while the Jewish state was to include much of northern Palestine together with the coastal lowlands from south of Tel Aviv to Haifa, and the Negev with the port of Eilat on the Gulf of Aqaba.

On the day the resolution was approved in New York the first Arab attack was made in Jerusalem; the Israelis were outnumbered, lacked heavy weapons, but fortunately for them the Arab armies were badly organized so the Jews were able to push them back on almost every front.[19]

The war, interspersed with truces and ceasefires, terminated on 29 December 1948 and Israel emerged with much more territory than originally allocated. A million Palestinian Arabs (Muslims and Christians, including Greeks, Armenians and other minorities) quitted Palestine, some being pushed out by the Jews; others, due to their fear of Jewish reprisals, leaving voluntarily. These refugees were housed in camps supported by the UN and by Arab states. Hatred of Israel and Zionism was deliberately fostered and since 1953 Israel has been in constant conflict with the 'people who refuse to be forgotten' – the Palestinians.

Today, after countless skirmishes and five wars (to date) there is still no peace in the Middle East.

Food in History

'If your enemy be hungry, give him bread to eat; and if he is thirsty, give him water to drink.'

Jewish Proverb

Israel is a melting pot of people. It is also 'a religious land, presumably the last religious land on earth'[1]. Yet she is more than all these for Israel is a new land with ancient dreams; a land where over a hundred tongues are slowly giving way to one – Hebrew, itself a new tongue based on the foundations of a much older tongue. In Israel the myriad customs, habits, morals, norms and traditions are being gently blended to produce a new society with its own unique culture.

When then can one commence with the history of Israeli food? With Abraham perhaps, but then he was not an Israeli and not even a Jew, but merely a Semite and must have eaten as did all the people in Mesopotamia where the food supply was frugal. The staple diet was bread – a crustless floury substance like polenta. Meals were eaten from a tray placed on the ground or on a low stool, very much as is the custom with the Bedouins of Arabia today; but then Abraham and his clan *were* Bedouins, who carried with them milk, dates, some flour, rice etc.

When in Egypt the Jews undoubtedly ate the same food as the ancient Egyptians. It was there that the ancestors of the modern Israelis first acquired the taste for 'falafel', 'ful medames' and 'melokhia soup'.

In Babylon the Jews followed the local customs of bread making. These breads were like lightly baked pancakes,

[1] quoted from *In King David's Footsteps* by Hans Habe.

the two sides of which separate in the heat of the oven – the modern version is the famed pita bread or, as it is better known in the Middle East, 'Khubz Arabi' – Arab bread. The Assyrian love of onions which were sold in strips and eaten raw, a custom still prevalent in Iran and Iraq, also produced the still popular Arab-Iranian bread with onions, 'Khubz Basali'. The Jews of Babylon drank beer – barley-based. They were permitted 1 gallon per person a month. They also drank wine – the famed palm tree wine which is still popular in certain regions of the Middle East, especially Iraq. The wine was produced by tapping the top of the trunk of the palm tree and collecting the sap which was then fermented, becoming very intoxicating after a few days.

Popular vegetables of the time were lentils, beans, barley, pumpkins, cucumbers and melons. There was very little meat, but abundant fish – both fresh and dried. Poultry, geese and duck were very popular too.

The Yemenite Jews, who emigrated to Israel in the 1940s, love baked desert locusts as did their ancestors in Babylon, who had a speciality of their own – 'locusts on skewers' or in modern terminology, 'locust kebabs'.

The early food of the Jews was primitive except on special occasions and the staple diet consisted mainly of vegetables such as garlic, leeks, onions and raw herbs.

During their years of exile, as they travelled from land to land, the Jews adopted and adapted the cuisines of those lands. From the Romans they took the art of preparing 'strudel' stuffed with honey and poppy seeds, and also baked honey and cheese cakes. From the Greeks they took 'sesame fried in oil'.

It is rarely appreciated today that before Christianity took root Judaism was a powerful force and was successfully converting the Roman world. Ancient governments whether Greek, Roman, Assyrian or Persian were not concerned with the thoughts or beliefs of their subjects, but only with their actions. So it can be safely assumed that the Jews of Asia Minor (St Paul was one of them) were not ethnically Jews, but only in belief, as were the Jews of Yemen, North Africa, and of Persia and Russia at a later date. Conversion does not instantly change the whole character, background and social habits of a people. An example of this is modern Turkey where about 90 per cent of the people, if not more, are of Greek, Armenian, Persian, Arab, Kurdish, Assyrian, Jewish and central European origin. The people of Syria, Egypt and North Africa, whose forefathers were converted to Islam, after 1400 years still retain a great number of their pre-Islamic characteristics and in particular their ancient foods, myths and physical characteristics. It is not surprising then to find the Jews of Russia looking like Russians or those of Yemen looking like the Yemenites for theirs was a religious bond, they have no ethnical unity.

It is only today in Israel that one can discern the beginnings of a new nation – predominantly made up of people of the Jewish faith. Yet the Israelis are not all Jewish. There are Muslims, Christians and people of minor sects all living there and rightfully claiming to be Israelis.

While under Arab domination, whether in Baghdad, Spain or Egypt, the Jews were Arabs of 'Jewish faith'. In Europe they were, in large part, Europeans (eg Poles, Russians, Tartars, Dutch etc) of 'Jewish faith' and therefore their food was that of the rest of the populace but with one very important exception. This was their observation of their 'religious' dietary laws, handed to them by Moses when he descended from Mount Sinai. He gave the women the code of culinary practice which they have followed ever since.

It is therefore only natural that Jews from Lithuania acquired the liking for the lowly herring, while in Spain and Portugal they acquired a liking for olives and olive oil as well as spices, peppers and the custom of frying fish in oil – a characteristic of pre-Muslim Middle Eastern cuisine dating, most probably, from the early Hittite and Greek colonization periods.

From Germany the Jews adopted sweet and sour stews; from Holland pickled cucumbers, butter and coffee cakes; from the Slavs of Poland and Russia many versions of borsht soup, soured cream dishes, blintzes, kasha, the fermented dark bread, smoked fish and fruit compôtes. From Rumania, Bulgaria and the Ottoman Empire they adopted stuffed vegetables and aubergine dishes; from Austro-Hungary the use of paprika, strudels and many tasty cakes.

Life was difficult for the Jew in the Christian lands. He was harassed and often persecuted. He lived in ghettos (a term originally used as the name for the geographical location of Venice Jewry). These ghettos, whether compulsory or not, enjoyed wide autonomy. They had their own officials, shops, guilds and law courts, eg Jewish officials collected their taxes and paid them to the authorities. Since religion was the main source of survival with the dietary laws one of the main supports of that religion, it is understandable why most Jews were satisfied with the ghetto solution. 'Long before residence in a restricted quarter or ghetto was compulsory the Jews almost everywhere had concentrated in separate parts of the towns in which they lived.'[20]

In Muslim countries Jews were almost totally integrated into the social and cultural life of Arab and Persian society – bar their religion. In Muslim countries the Jews ate the same food as the locals, thus in Iran kebabs, yogourt, stews ('khoresh') and omelettes ('sabzis') were adopted while in Syria and Palestine kebabs ('mushwis'), stuffed vegetables ('mahshis'), wheat and meat mixtures ('kubbehs', 'tabouli' etc) were absorbed into the Jewish cuisine. From Turkey they adopted stuffed vegetables ('dolmas'),

savoury pastries ('boregs') and soups ('chorbas') while in
North Africa the varieties of vegetable stew with semolina
rice ('cous-cous') were as much a favourite with the Jews
as with the Berbers.

After the establishment of the State of Israel the people
of Jewish faith, whose cherished dream of a land of their
own had finally materialized, set about creating not only a
new nation, but a new culture, art, music, poetry, architecture etc. A people who, for 2000 years, had nur-
tured in their metabolism the desire for self-expression set
about achieving the dream of their fathers. And as it is
with all people of tremendous energy, ambition and
dormant genius the Israelis launched into the world of
gastronomic experimentation. No nation in modern history has set out, deliberately, to create a new cuisine as
have the Israelis.

The new Israeli Jews have discarded many of the
traditional dishes brought over by their parents and
grandparents from the colder lands of Europe. The young
today prefer a lighter diet of vegetables, fish and dairy
foods more in the Middle Eastern tradition. In the incredible mêlée that today exists in Israel with the Ashkenazim (European Jews) jostling with the Sephardim (Oriental Jews) for power and position, the casual visitor may get
an impression of pandemonium, but the sensitive observer
will soon discern the important issues and discard the
irrelevant and passing ones. George Mikes most aptly
expresses the Israeli phenomenon: 'A geographical mobil-
ity, a complete new notion. Sometimes Israel is a European country in the Middle East, on other occasions she is
a Mediterranean country and nothing to do with Europe;
then again she is part of the Middle East.'[21] Indeed, day
by day Israel is becoming more and more a Middle
Eastern land for after all a nation's culture and cuisine
depend more on her geographical position and relating
climate than on anything else.

Israel then is a Middle Eastern land, but 50 per cent of its population are not Middle Eastern and here, indeed, lies the future, for as East and West mix a new cuisine is created. A cuisine rich with 'Eastern flavour' but with the added touch, some call it sophistication, of the West.

This new Israeli cuisine is already emerging and although one is offered vast arrays of international food in the restaurants of Tel Aviv, Jerusalem etc and the visitor can choose between French, Italian, Hungarian, Bulgarian, Indian, Chinese, Yemenite and Arab restaurants with countless other national and international dishes, the true cuisine of Israel is being meticulously created in the kibbutzim (collective agricultural settlements) and by talented chefs such as Roger Debasque[22], Mordechai Drucker, Arnold Bunysh and other unknown chefs and ordinary housewives. Hans Habe makes an interesting point when he remarks 'Apart from a handful of restaurants and private houses the best food in Israel is served in kibbutzim . . . you eat what the kibbutz produces, tomatoes, cucumbers etc.'[23]

Kibbutz food is basically farmhouse fare, simple, filling and satisfying. A typical breakfast comprises a large selection of what is available from the fields. This usually includes tomatoes, cucumbers, radishes, fruit and preserves as well as home-baked bread, marinated herrings and eggs etc. Indeed, one of Israel's great contributions (I hasten to add – to date) was created in the kibbutzim. 'Salat Benoosach Hakibbutz' is a vast array of vegetables which is a virtual do-it-yourself operation where one is encouraged to mix vegetables and dressings to create one's own salads.

A typical dinner at a kibbutz is composed of such things as balls of yogourt, chicken liver pâté, pickled fish, roast chicken or beef. Fresh fruit is the most usual dessert.

Eating habits are the most representative national characteristic. It is accepted by most people that Israel's hotel dining-rooms are sometimes not up to international standards due mainly to lack of skilled staff and inadequate training. The amount of food, especially at breakfast time, offered in hotels is gargantuan – a throwback to the land's agricultural origins. A casual glance at the menus offered in the 'international hotels' shows the diversity and wealth of choice. The most popular European dishes are Spaghetti Aglio, Miami salad, Chacha, Gash Pacha, Boeuf Strogonoff, Escalope Cordon Bleu, Steak au Poivre, Osso Bucco and Crêpes Suzette. From Eastern Europe comes Hungarian Guvetch, Marmiteze (pieces of fat from the neck of the beef), Batracion (highly spiced Rumanian kebabs), Bulgarian tarator soup and aubergine cake as well as the famed Ashkenazim specialities such as Meat Blinis, Plava, Kishke (beef tripe with a flour and lard filling), Kreplach etc. 'You can eat well in Israel if you are prepared to pay a lot . . . it is in the medium price bracket that Israel fails . . . Almost all of the good, cheap restaurants are owned by Yemeni, Iraqi and other Arab Jews . . . genuine Arab restaurants in East Jerusalem and the West Bank have also become popular. Arab food is more suitable for the climate than those famous and often excellent dishes developed in the snows of Poland and Russia.'[24] These 'Arab' restaurants serve such classics as Hummus-bi-tahina, Falafel, Kubbeh, Sinia, Cous-cous, Sahlab, Fistuke Halabi etc.

Ordinarily, little meat is consumed by the average Israeli since meat is expensive and is mostly imported as a government monopoly according to the standards of Keshrut. Local mutton and lamb are very popular. Pork, contrary to many non-Israelis' expectations, is openly sold and is very popular. It is sold under the name of 'white steak'. Turkey is most often substituted for veal and the local poultry is plentiful and tasty. Goose, duck, dove and partridge are also very popular – the last two are often served in Arab restaurants.

The Israelis eat a lot of cheese and produce their own versions of most popular European varieties, eg cheddar, suisse bleu, camembert, creamed cottage cheese and Greek-style feta and haloumi etc. They also consume large amounts of pickles. They are specialists at pickling and most vegetables lend themselves to this form of preserving.

Middle Eastern sweets are very popular in Israel, especially baklava, kunafa and the superb oriental ice creams flavoured with pistachios, walnuts, almonds and 'gum Arabi' that hang like carcasses from the ceilings of the small Arab sweet shops in Jerusalem and which are served by carving portions with a sharp knife. 'If there is anything as Jewish as the garment trade it is perhaps the drink trade, which may seem surprising in a people as sober and as abstemious as the Jews. But their abstemiousness (from drink at least – if a Jew becomes intoxicated it is usually on food) was no doubt one of the reasons for their prominence in the trade, they never felt tempted to consume their own stock.'[25] Israelis, on the whole, prefer soft drinks such as the local 'Gazos' (aerated fruit juice) or carbonated 'Tempo' as well as American 'Coca Cola' and British 'Schweppes' which have, over the years, all but captured the local market. Israelis prefer beer to wine, so much so that the Government's official propaganda 'Wine makes your food taste better, a little brandy makes you merrier' has to date had little effect. Although some excellent wines and liqueurs are produced (eg 'Adom Atic', 'Avdat', 'Cabernet Sauvignon', 'Sabra' liqueur and 'Keylevich' vodka) and exported to Europe and the USA the drink industry is still in its infancy, but as with everything else in this new, dynamic land the specialists are methodically working towards their goal of producing an internationally appreciated and successful beverage industry.

Finally, for the Israeli cuisine the future is bright. An

abundance of vegetables, fruits, nuts and dairy produce, a diverse populace with rich traditions, the will to re-create the old and attempt the new enhances and encourages the emergence of a new and exciting cuisine.

The existence of Israel will not only speed up the emergence of the Middle East generally as a cultural and economic world power, but will most assuredly help to stimulate the emergence of a new and revitalized Middle Eastern cuisine. The centuries-old food of Arabs and Turks will be affected by the influx of new cooking techniques, utensils and ingredients that are being systematically experimented with today in Israel and will no doubt be adopted by the rest of the Middle East tomorrow.

Climatic, Social and Religious Influences

All Israel is responsible for one another.

Yiddish expression

Wedged as it is between sea and desert, Israel is influenced by two contending forces. In winter strong winds blow from the sea while in summer dust clouds blow from the east, ie the Arabian deserts. The most influential natural element is the desert which merges imperceptibly into the cultivated areas of both Israel and neighbouring Jordan.

Israel is within the subtropical zone, has a rainy season in winter and a scorching, dry season in summer. The rainfall varies, eg in the narrow strip of land along the Mediterranean it rains in appreciable quantities, while the north gets most and the south receives very little. The length of the rainy season and the amount of precipitation varies from year to year and hence droughts are quite frequent.

The rivers of Israel are small and seasonal and often carry water during the short rainy season.

The country is mountainous and much of it is limestone although traces of volcanic rock can be found near Galilee. The mountains rise to an average height of over 3,500 ft (5,641 ft in the highlands of Edom). Between them geological faults have produced deep valleys. The longest and deepest is the Jordan Valley which drops from 656 ft below sea level at the Sea of Galilee to 1,312 ft at the Dead Sea – which, incidentally, is the lowest point on the earth's surface.

Because of the highly pervious nature of the limestone that forms the greater part of Israel's surface, water is swiftly absorbed and large subterranean lakes are formed. It was only a decade or so ago that geologists located these vast reservoirs of water and surfaced them by mechanical means. This new supply of water has enriched the otherwise limited resources and enabled the agriculturalists to expand the arable lands and 'green the Negev'.

The Israel of the past was never the 'land of milk and honey'. The land was too poor in natural resources. What chemical wealth there was, such as the minerals of the Dead Sea and the phosphates of the Negev, could not be exploited in biblical times and only the copper mines in the Arava were important. The once-forested mountain regions had disappeared long ago – Solomon had to import cedar wood from Lebanon, wine from Cyprus, copper and gold from lands as far away as Ethiopia, Cilicia and north Syria. Agriculture was the mainstay of the economy. Grain grew in the valleys, fruit trees on the hills. A limited amount of grazing was possible in the marginal areas. Herbs and spices grew in the Jordan Valley.

'A land of wheat, and barley, and vines, and fig trees, and pomegranates; a land of oil olive, and honey.' (Deuteronomy 8, 8)

But everything depended on the rain which was often unreliable and then caused drought and famine.

The climate of the land forged, and is once again forging, the character of the people. Strong willed, individualistic, fatalistic and idealistic thus the people created the belief of Yehwah – God of the Hebrews. Yehwah deepened the bond between man and the soil when he declared:

For the land, whither thou goest in to possess it, is not as the land of Egypt . . .
But the land, whither you go to possess it, is a land of hills and valleys, and drinketh water of the rain of heaven:
A land which the Lord thy God careth for. The eyes of the Lord thy God are always upon it, from the beginning of the year even unto the end of the year.

Deuteronomy 11, 10–12

History has been cruel to the Jewish people. Twice they were wrenched from their homeland and were dispersed over the surface of the earth to live amongst Gentiles with different customs and strange tongues, yet never once did they sever their links with the land. Three times each day they prayed: 'Sound the great horn for our freedom; raise the ensign to gather our exiles, and gather us from the four corners of the earth . . . And to Jerusalem, thy city, return in mercy . . . rebuild it soon in our days as an everlasting building . . .' This deep supplication inspired a bold and new revival. From Europe – mainly Russia – came young, energetic and, above all, idealistic Jews to resettle in Palestine in order to re-link themselves with their ancestors. Thus the first Jewish village was founded, Pehah Tikva. Others followed. People of different social backgrounds, speaking, thinking and reacting in different manners and tongues, trickled to their former land. Some were driven by dreams, some to what they hoped was a final refuge, others came driven with biblical fervour.

They came to a land their spiritual ancestors had left over 2000 years ago. Most were not Jewish by blood, but only by conviction and belief. The land they found as they arrived in Jaffa had not altered much in those ensuing 2000 years. Yet it was not barren as some extreme Zionists wanted to believe. There were people there, cities and villages, and although backward by the then European standards it was one of the most advanced regions of the moribund Ottoman Empire of which it was a part.

The twentieth century, which has seen the rise of nationalism, also affected the Jews. Belief is not enough – there must be a land where one can freely practise one's belief. Such was to be Israel.

Today over 3 million Jews are Israelis. The land is physically changing, desperately trying to catch up to the twenty-first century. The green is spreading over the yellow and brown of the desert. New farms, forests, canals and cities have veined this ancient land. New cities have sprung up where once only camels rested and Bedouin slept.

A nation is re-born, a dead language is re-born and, most important of all, a new society is being formed. Yet at this moment Israel is riddled with dilemmas. Does it represent a nation, a creed, a people, a language?

First, Israel is a multi-racial society. Ethnically it is as diverse as the USA or Canada. Linguistically it is a dictatorship where Hebrew is forced on all and people of Russian, American, Arab etc backgrounds are made to forget, as soon as possible, their former cultures and languages. Culturally it is a mess – since the ancients left very little artistic heritage apart from their books and beliefs and here lies one of the most important Israeli dilemmas. 'As the Jews are not a race there is no racial solidarity among the Jews. The Jews are a people of the 3 great binding forces – race, religion and people – people is the weakest and religion the strongest.'[26] In the words of Hans Habe: 'Israel is a religious land, presumably the last religious land on earth.'

Religion dominates every aspect of the state, of society

and especially of the cuisine. I would once again like to quote an extract from Hans Habe's excellent book. 'Israel is a socialist democracy with a gastronomic dictatorship. No restaurateur is forced to cook kosher, but kosher cuisine is a feature of le bonton . . . once a restaurateur has decided on kosher cuisine, he has to put up with being watched over by a 007 from the Rabbinate, the Mashgiuch – a dream of a job . . . I knew I would have to do without pork in Israel, but to be forbidden to pour milk in my coffee after my steak dinner was a new experience. Anyone wanting to smoke a cigarette on the Sabbath certainly can't do so where people are eating. A.K. Baedeker is long overdue . . . the majority of Israelis, especially the young, reject the mixing of State law with religious law, but in the kitchen a minority (18 MP) hold sway.' He continues to argue that an entire corps of codes and traditions, which had been evolved for life in the diaspora and which was becoming inadequate even for that, was transferred intact to the Jewish State. 'Traditional Judaism (largely a product of exile) can only thrive in exile.'[27]

Apart from its economic and political problems Israel has far more serious social problems to overcome, most of which are based on centuries-old religious precepts. Some of these are:

1 No civil marriage.
2 A Jew cannot marry a non-Jew. A Cohenite cannot marry a divorced woman.
3 All matrimonial jurisdiction is in the hands of Rabbinical courts who act in a spirit which was outdated even at the time of Jesus.
4 Only kosher and, consequently, dearer meat is available.
5 The Sabbath brings public transport to a standstill. The zealots (Mizrachi) claim it is outrageous to break

the Sabbath, thus depriving the great majority of the people of their chosen way of life.

6 Some 15 per cent of the population 'are permitted to terrorize the rest, or impose a way of life on them which they resist'.

7 Israel has a Socialist-orientated government and a Capitalist economy.

8 Eastern Jews, ie from Oriental lands, are discriminated against by the minority of Western Jews, both socially and, to some degree, racially.

9 The Jewish mentality, even in the 'brave new land of Israel', is as conservative as it has been throughout their history.

Since religion has been the dominant factor in keeping the Jewish people together, this very religion has, over the centuries, evolved codes of behaviour that touch every aspect of a person's life and especially his social life, eg according to Jewish law all agricultural work must cease in the Sabbatical year (one in seven). If this ruling were to be strictly applied Israel would become bankrupt. The farmers, at least the great majority of them, have solved this problem by ignoring the law. Thus the Rabbinate sells the land to the Arabs for that year so that Jews can still work on it and eat the produce. Incidentally, the ultra-religious sects boycott Jewish produce and buy their vegetables from Arabs.

There are whole chapters in Leviticus devoted to health, cleanliness and social niceties, as well as permitted and 'taboo' foods. What then is a Jew permitted to eat or not to eat?

The dietary laws arising out of Mosaic Law are in themselves not too restrictive.

And every beast that pareth the hoof, that cleaveth the cleft into two claws, and cheweth the cud among the beasts, that ye shall eat. Nevertheless these ye shall not eat of them that chew the cud, or of them that divide the cloven hoof; as the camel and the hare and the coney; for they chew the cud, but divide not the hoof . . . And the swine, because it divideth the hoof, but cheweth not the cud . . . these shall ye eat of all that are in the waters, all that have fins and scales shall ye eat. And whatsoever hath no fins and scales ye may not eat.

Leviticus 11, 3–12

Moreover ye shall eat no manner of blood, whether it be of fowl or of beast in any of your dwellings. Whatsoever soul it be that eateth any manner of blood, even that soul shall be cut off from his people.

Leviticus 7, 26–27

Simply put a Jew is not permitted to eat pork, shellfish and, according to some authorities, turbot.

A major prohibition, 'thou shalt not seethe a kid in his mother's milk' (Deuteronomy 14, 21) has, through the ages, done more than most laws to complicate matters in a Jewish kitchen and as a result most Jewish homes have two sets of cutlery and crockery – one for meat dishes and one for milk-based preparations. Some families go even further by building two kitchen sinks while kosher catering establishments have to double up on everything, often to the extent of having two separate kitchens. To complicate matters further, two separate 'Passover dishes' are also kept by most 'practising' Jews thus culminating in four sets of cutlery and crockery!

The Rabbis evolved a method of slaughter and preparation to drain the meat of blood.[28] Other Semitic races, eg the Arabs, also practise a similar method where the throat of the animal is cut and the blood drained.

A Jewish Orthodox person will never eat in a non-Jewish home, or even in other Jewish homes. In Israel, as well as Europe and the USA, many families have – as with most Jewish customs – learnt to compromise. They keep kosher homes, but eat non-kosher out. Indeed, a large number of Jews when eating out in restaurants or in non-Jewish homes choose fish, egg or vegetarian dishes. The young Israelis, as with Reform Jews, have virtually cast aside the entire corps of dietary laws and as the Hebrew proverb has it, have tended to argue that, 'what goes into the mouth is less important than what comes out'.

But the dietary laws were formulated over the centuries by the sages. In fact there is no other people and religion in the history of man that has developed and co-ordinated so thoroughly all aspects of the human condition. The Holy Books are filled with wisdom and experience. Every moment of a Jew's life is worked out down to the minutest detail. There are whole chapters devoted not only to dietary laws, but to hygiene; 'the hands should always be washed before leaving the toilet' or 'abstention from bathing is a sin' or even these two quaint niceties: 'one should never expectorate (spit) where people pass' and 'clothes worn during the day should not be worn during the night'.

It is in matters relating to the kitchen that the laws really come into force. How food should be cleaned, prepared and served are explained. 'He who denies himself proper food is a sinner.' 'One should not bite off a piece of food and return either it or the remaining portion to the dish, or give it to someone else – from the standpoint of both etiquette and health.'

Even the types of vegetables and meats were pre-scribed, eg 'salt sweetens meat', 'venison is the easiest flesh to digest', 'small fish in brine are good to eat after fasting' and 'vegetables eaten raw cause pallor'. The list is unending. I would like to quote a passage from Baba Bathra where the subject of breakfast is dealt with as a typical illustration of the care and scientific approach (for those days) of the Jewish dietary laws.

Breakfast is the most important meal of the day as it has thirteen advantages; it protects from heat, cold, wind, evil spirits; brightens the intellect of the fool; helps one win a law suit; helps one learn; helps one teach; makes his words listened to and retained by his listeners; his flesh does not give excessive heat (causing him to perspire needlessly); makes him have affection for his wife and not lust after a strange woman; and it also kills intestinal parasites. To these some add it removes jealousy and substitutes love.

Festive Dishes

1 *Sabbath*

The Sabbath is the day of rest; all work is forbidden. The housewife also takes a holiday from the culinary department of the home and any hot meal consumed on that day must be prepared on Friday.

From this 'religious' law was created the 'Cholent', which over the ages was designed both to survive its long stay in the oven and also to make an expensive commodity – meat – go a long way. There are several recipes for this dish but the classic one was composed of fat brisket of beef, haricot and butter beans with onions, prunes and syrup. 'Kugel' dumplings (made of flour, grated potato, parsley, onion and chicken fat) were added on top and the whole thing was slowly (18–20 hours) cooked.

Another outstanding dish of the Sabbath is 'Gefilte fish', a must on all Sabbath tables and festive occasions, served with horseradish – plain or beet-coloured.

The third classic dish of the Sabbath is the famed 'Challah' – light, white bread made with eggs and glazed on the outside with egg yolks. The dough was intricately plaited and elongated in shape. There are several types of Challah – round ones, ladder-shaped ones (for the New Year, to symbolize the hopes and aspirations with which one was expected to approach the season).

Some other musts on the Sabbath were (and still are with a majority of European and American Jewry), chopped beef, liver, chicken soup to which 'noodles' are often added, eg 'Lokshen' or 'Mandlen', lamb breasts stuffed with rice, or roast shoulder of lamb; then several kinds of salad such as beet salad or pickled beet relish or 'Risi-bisi', green beans and almonds etc.

The Sabbath meal has become imbued not only with tradition but a greater aura of religious fever. The lady of the house lights two Shabbos candles, covers her head and says a prayer (brocha). Thus she brings into the house the Sabbath. The man of the house then fills a glass with wine and says 'brocha' over it. He takes a sip and passes it round for everyone else to sip. The bread is now blessed. The father breaks off pieces from the whole challah and takes one for himself then passes a piece to each member of the family.

If the Sabbath has its special dishes, so does almost every other occasion in the Jewish calendar.

2 Rosh Hashonah – 'the first day of creation'
In Israel Rosh Hashonah is a one-day holiday. It is celebrated with feasting as well as prayer (in keeping with the words of the prophet Nehemiah, 'Eat of the fat and drink the sweet.')

In Babylon the main course of the feast was a whole sheep's head (symbolizing 'the head of the year'). Another custom, acquired most probably from Persia and symbolizing sweetness for the coming year, is to serve a bowl of honey and a plate of apple slices.

Another food custom acquired from Europeans (Poles and Rumanians) is to serve a Tzimmes, a sweet combination of carrots, potatoes and meat, cooked with sugar or honey to a rich golden colour. In short, Rosh Hashonah dishes are sweet based, and there are many variations of tzimmes dishes: eg prune and potato tzimmes, prune and rice tzimmes, tzimmes knaidle etc. Then there are sweet-based biscuits such as 'Tayglach' – which are dough covered in a honey, sugar and ginger mixture, with a nut and raisin filling – 'Tayglach mit Neshomas.'

The Rosh Hashonah celebrations culminate in the fast of Yom Kippur when one recalls one's failings during the past year and promises to improve in the coming year. 'We have trespassed, we have dealt treacherously, we have robbed; we have slandered, we have acted perversely and we have wrought wickedness' etc. Each prayer has its own melody; some are sung by the chazan, some by the congregation.

3 *The Passover*

Perhaps the most important festival in all the Jewish calendar is the Passover (or more precisely the Passover 'seder' which is the ceremonial meal celebrated on the first two nights of the festival).

Passover, in essence, celebrates the genesis of the Jewish people. It reminds them of their exodus from Egypt, their wanderings in the desert, the granting of the Torah (the written law transmitted to Moses on Mount Sinai, together with the oral law, later committed to writing). Bread is banished from the table to be replaced by 'Matzo' (unleavened bread).

And they baked unleavened cakes of the dough which they brought forth out of Egypt, for it was not leavened: because they were thrust out of Egypt and could not tarry, neither had they prepared for themselves any victual.

Exodus 12, 39

No leavened breadcrumbs are allowed to remain in the house. The whole dwelling is springcleaned and all the leavened foods burned.

The Seder (it means 'order') is part banquet, part prayer meeting with its own liturgy – the Hagadah. The first Seder was celebrated by the Israelites after the Exodus from Egypt. During the festive ritual each of the symbols are explained so that the children learn and understand. The symbols are the following:

Afikomen – three whole matzos in the folds of a napkin.

Roast lamb bone – symbolizing the sacrifice brought to the Temple by each family.

Hard-cooked eggs – placed in the shell against an open flame to roast on one side.

Bitter herbs (Morar) – grated horseradish, unflavoured and unseasoned. During the service some of the morar is placed between two small pieces of matzo and passed to each person around the festive table.

Charoses – chopped nuts and grated apples moistened with wine and flavoured with cinnamon.

Hard-cooked egg and salt water – sliced or diced hard-boiled eggs are placed in one dish of the Seder Plate and salt water in another. The Plate is served to each person during the service as a symbol of life's burdens and hopes of overcoming them.

Greens and salt water – parsley, chicory, lettuce or watercress or other available greens are the symbols of hope and redemption. The greens are dipped in the salt water during the service.

Wine – specially prepared wine for Passover is served in goblets that are refilled four times during the Seder service. Today some Israelis refill a fifth time as a symbol of Israel's statehood.

Cup of Elijah – a special goblet of wine is placed on the table towards the end of the service and the door is opened for the 'Coming of Elijah', symbolizing the hope for a more perfect world of justice and joy for all.

During the week of Passover, meals vary from the rest of the year. All vegetables, except peas and beans, are used. Bread is replaced by matzo, matzo meal or potato flour. Meat, poultry and fish are permitted as well as all kinds of drinks so long as they are labelled 'for Passover use' and all fruits, fresh or tinned.

The uniqueness of the Jewish cuisine comes to the fore in the Passover cuisine, for the Jewish housewife was obliged to use her ingenuity and imagination to create tasty and interesting dishes.

The use of matzo bread and matzo meal has developed a great repertoire of dishes that are uniquely Jewish. Perhaps the only Jewish cuisine is the Passover cuisine, created by history, religion and climatic circumstances, but with religion dominating all. Typical Passover dishes are – all matzo and matzo products as well as chremzlach, knaidlach (dumplings), Passover bagels, special Passover omelettes, carnatzlach (small sausages), meat-filled latkes, Passover blintzes (pancakes) etc.

4 *Purim*

The Book of Esther tells the story of Purim, how a bad vizir, Haman, tried to destroy the Jews of Persia and how his efforts were foiled by the intervention of Queen Esther and Mordechai (a court Jew). The entire book is read out in the synagogue on the eve of the festival and on the following morning. Children whistle, clatter and stamp their feet every time the name of Haman is mentioned. Purim is the one time, perhaps, when a pious Jew drinks to get drunk or, as the proverb says 'until one doesn't know Mordechai from Haman'.

Purim has its special foods. The Homentaschen may be filled with poppy seeds, honey and fruit, nuts and raisins. They are sometimes three-cornered or shaped like donkey's ears or elongated. There are gingerbread men – little Hamans etc.

5 *Channukah*

The Festival of Lights is one of the happiest holidays, celebrated by Jews all over the world. It was first commemorated by Judas Maccabee in the year 165 B.C. and since then Jews have gathered round the candelabrum (Menorah) lighting one candle on the first night, two on the second and so on until the final night of Channukah.

Traditional Channukah food customs include the eating of latkes, kugelach or kugel as well as a roast of chicken, goose, duck or, especially in Israel, turkey.

Foodlore gives us the origin of latkes at Channukah time as being the period when the Battle of Maccabees was at its height and the women mixed batter and fried flat cakes called latkes. The grated-potato latkes was a variation developed in Central Europe centuries later. Soofganiyah (doughnuts filled with jam) have become a very popular Channukah food in Israel today.

Also in present-day Israel, to the rich, traditional festive dishes are being added new ones – some borrowed from other nations, others being created from the 'milk and honey' of the land but all contributing to what will be, in a few generations' time, a genuine 'Israeli cuisine'. What a pity that we cannot live long enough to see such transformation of a culture. What a pity we cannot all be Methuselahs. Yet let us live these 'seven score years of ours in Peace and Good Health and Shalom to all'.

Shalom, shalom to one and all. Remember the concluding words of the Talmud: 'the Lord will give strength to His people . . . the Lord will bless His people with peace'. (Psalm 29, 2).

Let us add: Mazeltov!

NOTES

1 'People of various sorts joined them in great numbers; there were flocks too and herds in immense droves.' Exodus 12, 38

2 Egyptians called their country Kemit (black). Kam in Hebrew means black, heat or burnt. The inhabitants of Egypt were the black (ham, kam or cham) of the Bible.

'If the Biblical version is even slightly accurate, how could the Jewish people be free of Negro blood? In 400 years it grew from 70 to 600,000 in the midst of a negro nation that dominated it throughout the period . . . At present it seems almost certain that Moses was an Egyptian, therefore a negro.' *African Origin of Civilisation*, Cheikh Anta Diop, Lawrence Hill & Co., USA 1976

3 Jethro was a Midianite priest whose seven daughters served as his shepherds. Moses married Zipporah. Jethro advised Moses on the reorganization of the judicial system and his name is confused with Hobeds and Reuel in Judaic writings.

4 *Peace in the Holy Land*, J.B. Glubb, Hodder and Stoughton, London, 1971

5 Ibid.

6 Some of the Greek cities were Antioch, Selucid, Latakia, Acre (Ptolemais), Jaffa (Joppa), Ashdod (Azotus), Gaza, Rafa (Raphia), Sabaste (Samaria which had been rebuilt as a Greek city) and Ammon (Amman).

7 Glubb, op. cit.

8 *War of the Jews*, Josephus, Penguin Books Ltd, London, 1959

9 A man named Bar Kokhba was hailed as the Messiah by Rabbi Akiba (a much loved and respected teacher). The revolt was brutally suppressed. Rabbi Akiba was killed, Jerusalem was renamed Aelia Capitolina and Jews were excluded from its walls.

10 Glubb, op. cit.

11 'The Jews were everywhere the object of popular insult and oppression . . . though protected, it must be confessed, by the laws, the Church, as well as, in general by the temporal Princes.' *Europe during the Middle Ages*, H. Hallam.

There were three basic causes for this anti-Jewish attitude:

a) Jews were money lenders and tax collectors;

b) They were unsociable, refused to join public festivals or eat and drink with Christians;

c) Their 'real or imagined' contempt for Gentiles since they alone were the chosen people.

12 *Jewish Life in the Middle Ages*, Israel Abraham, London, 1932

13 In 1391 alone 200,000 Jews were massacred and many others were forcibly converted. These converts were called

Marranos and many rose to very high positions. Many
Marranos still practised Judaism in secret.

14 *The Jews*, Chaim Bermant, Weidenfeld and Nicolson,
London, 1972

15 Glubb, op. cit.

16 In 1781 Austria opened the doors of universities and
academies to Jews. In 1789 the French Revolution abo-
lished all religious disabilities.

17 Keren Kayemethle–Israel, founded in 1901. It is responsible
for land development in Israel, eg the opening up of the
Jazreel and Hula valleys, the Jerusalem corridor and the
northern Negev.

The J.N.F.S. vast afforestation programme has also been
greatly changing the face of the land.

18 The Zionist terrorists organized thefts from British depots,
blew up railways and bridges. The Irgun blew up the King
David Hotel in 1946. It was the headquarters of the
Mandatory Government.

19 This Zionist interpretation must be taken with a small pinch
of salt since only two 'Arab' armies were drawn into serious
fighting against newly established Israel and the total of
Arab forces in May 1948 was approximately 20,000, while
the Jewish strength was reckoned to be somewhere in the
region of 62,500.

(Palmach 3,500, Hagana 55,000, Irgun 4,000).

20 Abraham, op. cit.

21 *Israel Today and Tomorrow*, George Mikes, André
Deutsch, London, 1969

22 There are nearly 600 kibbutzim and moshavim (co-oper-
ative agricultural farms) in Israel. They contain 3 per cent of
the population, but have an influence out of all proportion
to their numbers. They produce nearly half the agricultural
products of the country and have, over recent years,
expanded into small-scale industrial enterprises, eg hotels,
restaurants, electronics etc.

23 *In King David's Footsteps*, Hans Habe, W.H. Allen,
London, 1973

Israel's present-day agricultural produce is extremely
varied. Bananas, avocados, guavas, sugar beet as well as the
traditional citrus fruits, apples, dates etc have been successfully produced and indeed one of the most successful export
industries is that of fruit and vegetables.

24 Mikes, op. cit.
25 Bermant, op. cit.
26 Ibid.
27 Habe, op. cit.
28 Shechita, the ritual method of slaughtering animals for food, is accepted by all today to be the most humane as it induces, most rapidly and reliably, complete anaemia of the brain with loss of consciousness; also the cutting of the tissues with a sharp knife is relatively painless.

Appetizers and Salads

Appetizers and Salads

SALAT BENOOSACH HAKIBBUTZ	*Kibbutz salad*
HUMMUS	*Chickpeas with tahina*
FALAFEL	*Chickpea rissoles*
SALAT ZALOUK	*Cooked vegetable salad*
TOURETO	*Cucumber and bread salad*
BEITZA MIMRAKH	*Egg and horseradish dip*
HATZAY AGVANIYOK IM AVOCADO	*Tomatoes stuffed with avocado*
SALAT KROOV	*Cabbage salad*
SALAT PILCHEI AVOCADO GEZER BENITZ TAPUZIM	*Avocado, carrot and orange salad*
SALAT SELEK	*Beetroot salad*
TAPOOZ IM SALAT-ZEYTIM	*Orange and olive salad*
MILON BTZLOCHIT	*Melon cups*
MATOK MARIR KADOUREY BASAR	*Sweet and sour meatballs*
KOBBE M-MATZO	*Matzo kibbeh*
SHAKSHOUKA	*Eggs in tomato sauce*
COCKTAIL DAGIM	*Jaffa cocktail*
GEHAKTE LEBER	*Chopped liver*

GEHAKTE HERRING	*Chopped herring salad*
DAG-MALOOLAH IM TAPOUZIM	*Herrings with apples*
TABOULI	*Cracked wheat salad*

APPETIZERS AND SALADS

Israelis are fast becoming vegetarians. Scores of health food shops, vegetarian cafés and restaurants have sprung up all over the country in recent years. The kibbutzim were always vegetarian-minded and understandably so, since they grow the finest fruits and vegetables in the land and are the first to profit from the toil of their labour.

The European Jews – Ashkenazim – were brought up with cabbage, potatoes and, of course, fish. The latter was served in various ways: as soup, patties, stuffed, pickled, fried, sweet and sour, in aspic etc. This love of fish, particularly herring, is still strong in Israel and there are some excellent fish restaurants in Tel Aviv and Jerusalem.

'When you have no fish, make do with herring – it's also fish!' – so said the old-timers, but it appears the young Israelis (Sabras) prefer lighter and simpler food. They have also taken a liking to the indigenous Palestinian Arab dishes, notably hummus and falafel, both made with chickpeas and sold throughout the length and breadth of Israel in cafés, snackbars and restaurants. However, truer versions of these and most 'Arab' salads and appetizers should be bought from Arab shops since their Jewish versions lack authenticity. There is, for example, a restaurant in Jerusalem claiming to be 'Malak Hummus' – 'King of Hummus'; however, king or not, it serves the worst hummus I have ever eaten!

We start this chapter with what is perhaps the truest embodiment of Israel – the kibbutzim and a salad popularized by them.

SALAT BENOOSACH HAKIBBUTZ
Kibbutz salad

The kibbutzim is the creator of a salad now popularized throughout Europe and North America. It is an array of vegetable salads like those listed below, as well as Cos lettuce and fresh herbs such as tarragon, mint, parsley and basil. Also often included are sliced, cooked beetroot, hard-boiled eggs, anchovy fillets, chopped pickled herrings etc – in fact, anything available. The list is very long, but the idea is simple. Namely, mix and season to your personal choice and taste. I have listed several typical combinations, but leave you to create some of your own. Quantities are not included since this type of salad is best suited to large groups, eg parties, buffets or, as in Israel, outdoor eating.

Fennel
Raisins
Celery seeds
Lemon juice
Olive oil

1 Grate the fennel, add the raisins and season with the celery seeds, lemon juice and olive oil.

Tangerines
Mayonnaise
Cinnamon
Chopped hazelnuts

1 Divide the tangerines into segments.
2 Mix the mayonnaise with the cinnamon and hazelnuts.
3 Dress the tangerines with this mixture.

Cucumber
Yogourt
Dried mint, finely chopped

1 Slice the cucumber, add the yogourt and sprinkle with the dried mint.

Leeks
Black olives
Radishes, sliced
Lime juice
Olive oil
Chopped tarragon

1 Wash and slice the leeks into a bowl, add all the remaining ingredients and mix well.

Tomatoes
Chopped parsley
Olive oil
Sumak powder

1 Slice the tomatoes and sprinkle with the parsley, olive oil and sumak.

Onions, sliced into rings
Pimientoes, chopped
Olive oil and lemon juice
Salt
Oregano

1 Arrange the onion rings on a plate.
2 Mix the pimientoes, olive oil, lemon juice, salt and oregano together and pour over the onions.

Serve each salad in a separate salad bowl as part of a large salad tray. Garnish with extras of Cos lettuce, herbs, spring onions etc. and serve with pita bread.

HUMMUS
Chickpeas with tahina

One of the great appetizers of the Middle East, hummus is very popular throughout Israel although, of course, it is of Syrian origin. In any self-respecting restaurant you are offered hummus (with the emphasis on the h, pronounced kh), which is eaten with pita bread.

Hummus will keep for several days in the refrigerator and so you can make a substantial amount, but do not add the garlic and other spices until just before serving.

> 450 g (1 lb) chickpeas, soaked overnight in cold water
> 3 cloves garlic, peeled
> 300 ml (½ pint) tahina
> 1 teaspoon chilli pepper
> 3 teaspoons salt
> 2 teaspoons ground cumin
> Juice of 2 lemons

For Garnish:
A little red pepper, cumin, olive oil, lemon juice, chopped parsley and reserved chickpeas

1 Rinse the chickpeas under cold running water and then place them in a large saucepan three-quarters filled with cold water.
2 Bring to the boil and then lower the heat and simmer until the chickpeas are tender.
3 From time to time remove the scum which will appear on the surface and add more water if, and when, necessary.
4 Drain the chickpeas into a sieve and wash very thoroughly under cold running water.
5 Set aside 2–3 tablespoons of chickpeas to use as a garnish.
6 Using a liquidizer, reduce the chickpeas to a thick

paste or purée. You can add a little water to facilitate the liquidization, but not too much or the purée will become too thin.

7 While liquidizing the chickpeas add the cloves of garlic – this will ensure that they are properly ground and evenly distributed.

8 Transfer the purée to a large bowl.

9 Add the tahina, chilli pepper, salt, cumin and lemon juice and mix in very thoroughly.

10 Taste and adjust the seasoning to your own satisfaction.

11 To serve, either divide the mixture between individual bowls or pour into a large serving dish. Smooth the hummus with the back of a soup spoon from the centre out to the edges so that there is a slight hollow in the centre. Decorate in a star pattern with alternating dribbles of red pepper and cumin. Pour a little olive oil and lemon juice into the centre and then garnish with a little chopped parsley and the whole chickpeas.

FALAFEL
Chickpea rissoles

'Traditional best-loved treats are falafel and shawarma. Falafel is like a sandwich made from balls of deep-fried ground chickpeas plus chopped salad and pickles, with a dollop of tahina sauce and an additional dollop of super-hot sauce all inside a round and hollow Arab bread called pita.'

Melting-Pot Cookery

Falafel may be 'traditional' as far as Israel is concerned for the past thirty years or so, but it has been eaten by Arabs and Jews of the Middle East for thousands of years. It is indeed one of Egypt's national dishes dating from the days of the mighty Pharaohs.

450 g (1 lb) cooked chickpeas
90 ml (3 fl oz) water
1 egg, lightly beaten
1 teaspoon salt
½ teaspoon black pepper
½ teaspoon turmeric
2 tablespoons chopped fresh coriander leaves, or
    parsley
½ teaspoon cumin
½ teaspoon cayenne pepper
1 clove garlic, crushed
1 tablespoon tahina paste, or olive oil
50 g (2 oz) fresh white breadcrumbs
50 g (2 oz) flour
Oil for deep frying

1 Pass the chickpeas twice through a mincer into a large
  mixing bowl.
2 Add the water, egg, salt, pepper, turmeric, coriander
  leaves, cumin, cayenne pepper, garlic, tahina paste or
  olive oil, and the breadcrumbs.
3 With your hands, combine all the ingredients into a
  soft, but firm mixture.
4 Form the mixture into walnut-sized balls and coat
  them with the flour.
5 In a large pan, heat the oil until it reaches 182°C
  (360°F) on a deep-frying thermometer, or until a small
  cube of stale bread dropped into the oil browns in
  about 50 seconds.
6 Add the rissoles to the oil, a few at a time, and fry
  them for about 3 minutes until they are evenly
  browned.
7 Remove the rissoles from the oil, drain on kitchen
  paper and keep warm while the remainder are cooking.
8 Serve hot.

SALAT ZALOUK
Cooked vegetable salad

This is a North African salad, spicy and rich. It has become very popular with the Israelis especially since some of the finest and most reasonable eating houses are run by Moroccans or Tunisians. It can be kept for several days in a refrigerator and it makes a very tasty appetizer. It is normally eaten with bread – pita or crusty bread of your choice.

> 2 medium aubergines, cut into 1 cm (½ in) cubes
> 3 courgettes, cut into ½ cm (¼ in) slices
> 7 tablespoons vegetable oil
> 1 teaspoon cayenne pepper
> 2 cloves garlic, crushed
> 1 teaspoon salt
> Water
> 3 red or green peppers, sliced
> 3 large tomatoes, blanched, peeled and chopped
> 2 chillies, seeded and finely chopped

1 Place the aubergines, courgettes, oil, pepper, garlic and salt in a large saucepan.
2 Pour in enough water to just cover the vegetables.
3 Bring to the boil, cover, lower the heat and simmer for 10 minutes.
4 Uncover and add the peppers, tomatoes and chillies.
5 Cook, uncovered, stirring occasionally until all the water has evaporated and the vegetables are tender.
6 Remove from the heat and leave to cool.
7 Serve cold with bread.

TOURETO
Cucumber and bread salad

Better a morsel of bread and peace with it, than a house full of feasting, with strife.

Hebrew Proverb

This is a simple and economical dip of Sephardic origin. It makes an ideal buffet table accompaniment.

   6 slices of bread
   Water for soaking
   1 cucumber, peeled and chopped
   2 cloves garlic, crushed
   7 tablespoons olive oil
   Juice of 1 lemon
   ½ tablespoon salt
   ½ teaspoon white pepper
   1 teaspoon paprika
   1 teaspoon cumin

1 Cut off the bread crusts and discard.
2 Soak the bread in water and then squeeze dry.
3 Place the bread in a bowl and mix in the chopped cucumber, garlic, 5 tablespoons of the oil, the lemon juice and the salt and white pepper.
4 Purée this mixture in an electric blender. If necessary, add just a few drops of water to achieve a smooth result.
5 Pour the toureto into a shallow serving dish and chill for a few hours.
6 Just before serving mix the remaining oil with the paprika and cumin in a small cup.
7 Dribble the dressing over the toureto and serve.

BEITZA MIMRAKH
Egg and horseradish dip

For the worm, nothing is sweeter than horseradish

Proverb

This is a popular dip, particularly with Ashkenazim Jews. It can be served as part of a buffet or as an appetizer.

4 hard-boiled eggs
300 ml (½ pint) soured cream
50 g (2 oz) freshly grated horseradish
1 tablespoon prepared mustard
1 tablespoon lemon juice
1 teaspoon sugar
1 teaspoon salt

1 Finely chop the hard-boiled eggs and place in a mixing bowl.
2 Add the remaining ingredients and mix gently. Spoon into a bowl and chill until ready to serve.
3 Eat with bread or matzo biscuits.

HATZAY AGVANIYOK IM AVOCADO
Tomatoes stuffed with avocado

Stuffed vegetables are a very old tradition in the Middle East, but the concept of using avocado and cheese in tomatoes and eggs is relatively new as well as being very attractive.

4 tomatoes
2 small ripe avocados or 1 large one
½ teaspoon salt
½ teaspoon black pepper
½ teaspoon horseradish sauce
1 teaspoon finely chopped parsley
4 eggs, hard-boiled

225 g (½ lb) grated cheese eg feta, stilton or lancashire
1 teaspoon onion, finely chopped
6–8 black olives, stoned and chopped
½ teaspoon paprika

For garnish:
Watercress
Green olives

1 Cut a thin slice off the top of each tomato and then scoop out and reserve the pulp, taking care not to damage the tomato shells.
2 Put the tomato pulp into a bowl.
3 Peel the avocados, mash well and add to the tomato flesh.
4 Add the salt, pepper, horseradish and parsley and mix together.
5 Taste and adjust seasoning if necessary and then fill the tomatoes with this mixture.
6 Set aside in the refrigerator while you prepare the eggs.
7 Peel the eggs and cut them in half lengthways.
8 Remove the yolks and place in a bowl.
9 Mash the yolks, add the cheese, onion and black olives, and mix well.
10 Season with a little salt to taste.
11 Divide this mixture between the halves of egg, reserving a little for garnish.
12 Sprinkle the eggs with the paprika.
13 Arrange the watercress on a large platter and place the remaining cheese mixture in the centre.
14 Arrange the stuffed tomatoes and eggs around the platter, garnish with the green olives and serve.

SALAT KROOV
Cabbage salad

'The olive tree that stands in silence
Upon the hills of time.
The voices echo in the valley
As bells of evening chime.'

Jewish folk poem

This is a colourful and refreshing salad which makes a wonderful accompaniment to all kinds of roast or grilled meat.

¼ red cabbage, finely shredded
¼ green cabbage, finely shredded
1 small onion, sliced into rings
2 spring onions, thinly sliced, including heads
150 ml (¼ pint) mayonnaise
½ teaspoon sugar
1 tablespoon lemon juice
½ teaspoon salt
¼ teaspoon black pepper
About 15 black olives
About 15 green olives
2 cooked beetroot, thinly sliced
2 tablespoons blanched almonds, slivered

1 Combine the cabbage and onion together in a salad bowl.
2 Mix the mayonnaise, sugar, lemon juice, salt and pepper together in a small bowl.
3 Pour this dressing over the vegetables and mix well.
4 Add the olives, beetroot and almonds and toss lightly.
5 Chill for about 1 hour and serve.

SALAT PILCHEI AVOCADO GEZER BENITZ TAPUZIM
Avocado, carrot and orange salad

A sophisticated-looking yet extremely simple salad which makes an excellent hors d'oeuvre. This dish has already acquired a fame for itself far beyond Israel. It was served to me in, of all places, a chic restaurant in downtown Dusseldorf.

> 225 g (½ lb) carrots, grated
> 120 ml (4 fl oz) orange juice
> ¼ teaspoon chilli pepper
> ¼ teaspoon grated root ginger
> ½ teaspoon salt
> 1 large ripe avocado, chilled
> Juice of 1 lemon
> 2 tablespoons seedless raisins

1 Put the grated carrot in a bowl.
2 Add the orange juice, pepper, ginger and salt and toss thoroughly.
3 Refrigerate the salad for 1–2 hours.
4 When ready to serve cut the avocado in half, loosen the seed and lift it out with the tip of a knife.
5 Strip off the skin carefully.
6 Now cut each avocado half into 2 lengthways.
7 Place each section on a small serving dish and sprinkle with lemon juice.
8 Pile the carrot into the cavities of the avocado quarters.
9 Sprinkle the raisins over the top.
10 Pour any of the remaining orange marinade over the segments and serve immediately.

Serves 4

SALAT SELEK
Beetroot salad

All olive-oil-based salads are from the Mediterranean
region. This kibbutz-based salad is no exception. It com-
bines the simple lightness of the Orient with the more
intriguing flavour of Central Europe by the clever use of
chicory. It can be served on a buffet table (which it often
is) or as an accompaniment to meat and poultry dishes.

> 4 whole cooked beetroot, peeled
> 2 heads of chicory, coarse and discoloured outer leaves
>   discarded
> 3–4 spring onions, chopped
>
> *For the dressing:*
> 1 tablespoon lemon juice
> 1 tablespoon vinegar
> ½ teaspoon salt
> ¼ teaspoon black pepper

1 Slice the beetroot thinly into a salad bowl.
2 Tear the chicory leaves into bite-sized pieces and add
  to the bowl together with the spring onions.
3 Mix the dressing ingredients together and pour over
  the salad. Toss lightly and serve.

Serves 6–8

TAPOOZ IM SALAT-ZEYTIM
Orange and olive salad

Israelis make clever use of their commodities such as
avocado, grapefruit and, of course, the famed 'Jaffa'
oranges.

This salad is similar to the well-known Arab orange and
olive salad – 'munkazina'. Here however the onions have

been replaced by a liqueur. I do not recommend kirsch and prefer filfar – a Cypriot orange liqueur, or any other orange-based liqueur.

This is an excellent salad with veal and, dare I say it, pork!

    2 oranges, peeled and segmented
    50 g (2 oz) black olives, stoned and sliced
    50 g (2 oz) green olives, stoned and sliced
    ¼ teaspoon salt
    ¼ teaspoon cayenne pepper
    1 tablespoon olive oil
    ¼ teaspoon cumin
    2 tablespoons filfar (or kirsch, if unavailable)

1 Cut each orange segment into about 3 pieces.
2 Put them into a large bowl with the olives, salt, pepper, olive oil and cumin.
3 Mix them well together.
4 Sprinkle the liqueur over the top and stir.
5 Place in the refrigerator to chill.
6 Spoon into a serving dish and serve.

MILON BTZLOCHIT
Melon cups

'Which is the most tasty yet economical fruit?'
'Melons'.
'Why?'
'Because you eat the fruit, give your animal the skin, and the seeds – when roasted – give you endless days of leisurely munching.'

Palestinian saying

This is a colourful and decorative appetizer. In some form or other it appears on many Israeli restaurant menus, and deservedly so. It is so much more appetizing than plain melon, or melon with ham, or melon with one kind of liqueur or another.

2 cantaloupe melons
50 g (2 oz) cooked rice
75 g (3 oz) dates, stoned and chopped
1 avocado, flesh thinly sliced
50 g (2 oz) walnuts, shelled and coarsely chopped
2 tablespoons sultanas or raisins
4 green olives, diced
4 black olives, diced
½ teaspoon salt
Few grindings black pepper
1 tablespoon lemon juice

For garnish:
Lettuce leaves and sprigs of fresh mint or tarragon.

1 Cut the melons in half then remove and discard the seeds.
2 With a large spoon scoop out the flesh taking care not to damage the skin.
3 Cube the flesh.
4 In a large bowl mix the melon cubes with the rice.
5 Add the dates, avocado slices, nuts, sultanas and olives.
6 Season with the salt, pepper and lemon juice and toss very gently.
7 Line each melon shell with 2 or 3 lettuce leaves and then fill with the melon mixture.
8 Garnish with the mint or tarragon sprigs.
9 Chill for 30 minutes and then serve.

Serves 4

MATOK MARIR KADOUREY BASAR
Sweet and sour meatballs

Better known in Yiddish as 'Ziess un zoyere gehakte flaysh' this recipe is ever popular on most Hasidic dinner tables. It is similar to some of the meatball dishes of Russia and Poland and, strangely enough, not too different from those of Iran and Turkey (the source of most meatball recipes) – except that in these lands lamb is usually preferred to beef.

Although usually served as an appetizer these meatballs also make a fine main dish when served with potatoes or a pilav.

> 1 tablespoon oil
> ½ medium onion, finely chopped
> 450 g (1 lb) minced beef
> 1 thick slice bread, crusts removed
> 1 teaspoon salt
> ½ teaspoon black pepper
> 350 g (¾ lb) ripe tomatoes, blanched, peeled and
>   chopped
> 1½ tablespoons tomato purée
> 1.2 litres (2 pints) water
> 2 tablespoons lemon juice
> 2 tablespoons dark brown sugar

1 Heat the oil in a small pan and sauté the onion until golden. Turn into a mixing bowl and add the meat.
2 Soak the bread in 150ml (¼ pint) water, squeeze dry and add to the bowl.
3 Season with the salt and pepper and knead until the mixture is well blended and smooth. Dampen your hands with water from time to time.
4 Keeping your hands damp, form the mixture into walnut-sized balls.
5 Place the chopped tomatoes in a large saucepan with

the tomato purée and stir in the water, lemon juice and
sugar. Bring to the boil.
6 Add the meatballs, lower the heat and simmer for
about 45 minutes. Serve hot.

Serves 8 as an appetizer and 4 as a main meal

KOBBE M-MATZO
Matzo kibbeh

'Kibbeh' is a great classic of the Middle Eastern cuisine. It
is, perhaps, the most beloved dish of the Syrians and
Lebanese and there are many variations of it.

Basically 'kibbeh' is a mixture of burghul (cracked
wheat) and lean minced lamb. You can eat kibbeh raw
(kibbeh nayah), fried or grilled (kibbeh-bil-sanieh), or
stuffed with meat, nuts and spices (kibbeh tarablousieh).

Although traditionally made with burghul, over the
ages Oriental Jews have evolved their own particular
version of this dish and have substituted matzo meal for
the burghul. The kobbe m-matzo has become very popular today, not only with the resident Arabs and Jews, but
in a great number of restaurants and cafés catering for
people from all walks of life and different parts of the
world. These egg-shaped kibbeh are light and tasty and
will keep in the refrigerator for several days. The quantities given below will make about 12. One per person is
usually enough when served as an hors d'oeuvre, but 2 or
3 with a fresh salad make an ideal light meal.

225g (½ lb) matzo meal, medium
½ onion, finely chopped
3 tablespoons ground rice
1 teaspoon cumin
1 teaspoon salt
½ teaspoon black pepper

Water
Oil for frying

For the filling:
2–3 tablespoons oil
1 small onion, finely chopped
225 g (½ lb) minced lamb
2 tablespoons pine kernels, or chopped walnuts, or
    almonds
1 teaspoon salt
½ teaspoon black pepper
½ teaspoon allspice
2 tablespoons chopped parsley

For garnish:
Lemon wedges

1 First prepare the filling by frying the chopped onion in
  the oil until soft.
2 Add the remaining ingredients and cook over a gentle
  heat for 20–30 minutes, stirring frequently, until well
  cooked.
3 Remove from the heat and leave to cool.
4 To make the kibbeh put the matzo meal, onion,
  ground rice, cumin, salt and pepper together in a large
  bowl.
5 Adding a very little warm water at a time carefully
  knead with your hand to make a stiff dough.
6 To form the egg-shaped kibbeh you must keep your
  hands damp, so have a bowl of water to hand.
7 Take a lump of the kibbeh mixture about the size of a
  small tomato.
8 Hold it in one hand and, using the forefinger of your
  other hand, make a hole in the kibbeh.
9 Slowly widen the hole with your finger while gently

turning the kibbeh in the palm of the other hand until the shell is about ½ cm (¼ in) thick. If the shell cracks – as it often does with beginners, dip your fingers in the water and 'glue' the shell together again.

10 Place a tablespoon of the filling in the hole.

11 Wet your hands again and close the kibbeh, sealing up the hole with your fingers.

12 Roll the ball between your palms until you have a shape which approximates to an elongated egg.

13 Continue until you have used all the kibbeh and filling.

14 When ready to serve heat some oil in a saucepan and deep fry the kibbeh, 2 or 3 at a time, turning regularly until they are golden brown.

15 Remove from the oil, drain and then serve hot with wedges of lemon.

Makes 12 kibbeh

SHAKSHOUKA
Eggs in tomato sauce

One day Husham, the classic idiot of Ashkenazim humour, was asked 'Tell us how many eggs you can eat on an empty stomach?'

Husham thought for a long time then replied 'Five.'

'Stupid fool,' mocked the others, 'when you have eaten one egg your stomach is not empty any more!'

Husham laughed at himself – with them and thought this was a clever joke.

Just then a friend passed by. Husham confronted him and asked, 'How many eggs can you eat on an empty stomach?'

'Four,' said the friend.

Husham was annoyed. 'Shame,' he said, 'great shame.'

'Why?' asked the friend.

'Well, if you had guessed five I'd have had a clever answer for you!'

This recipe, originally from North Africa and which the wandering Jews picked up (like most other dishes) on their way home, has now become standard fare. It appears in virtually all cafés and restaurants because it is simple and cheap to prepare.

There are many versions. The one below I particularly like and the recipe was kindly given to me by the chef of a small family-run café in Jerusalem.

Serve with pita bread as an appetizer; on toast for breakfast; or even with a pilav for a light lunch or supper.

4 tablespoons oil
1 large onion, finely chopped
1 clove garlic, finely chopped
1 red pepper, thinly sliced
675 g (1½ lb) ripe tomatoes, blanched, peeled and
    chopped
½ teaspoon salt
6 eggs
Salt and black pepper

For garnish (optional):
½ teaspoon cayenne pepper or cumin powder

1 Heat the oil in a large frying pan, add the onion, garlic and red pepper and sauté until the onion is light golden.
2 Add the chopped tomatoes, including their liquid, and the salt. Stir well, cover and simmer for about 20 minutes.
3 Remove the cover, break the eggs over the surface and stir gently just to break the yolks. Replace the cover and cook for 3–4 minutes or until the eggs are set.

4 Sprinkle the eggs with a little salt and pepper (or use cayenne pepper or cumin powder) and serve.

COCKTAIL DAGIM
Jaffa cocktail

This is one of those new Israeli recipes that are gaining popularity due to their ingenuity in exploiting the particular tastes of the people. It is a very sophisticated cocktail which is extremely attractive, created by the well-known chef Mordechai Drucker who was originally from Poland – hence perhaps the penchant for things fishy!

2 carrots, peeled and sliced
1 onion, sliced
½ teaspoon salt
¼ teaspoon white pepper
110 g (4 oz) cod
110 g (4 oz) hake
110 g (4 oz) filleted fish eg haddock
2 pickled cucumbers, cut into ½ cm (¼ in) cubes
Capers

For the dressing:
120 ml (4 fl oz) mayonnaise
1½ liqueur glasses of brandy
Juice of 1 lemon

For garnish:
3 tablespoons tomato ketchup
6 slices of lemon

1 Half fill a medium saucepan with water and bring to the boil.

2 Add the carrot and onion slices, salt and pepper and boil vigorously for 5 minutes.
3 Lower the heat, add the fish and simmer for 20 minutes.
4 Remove from the heat; using a slotted spoon transfer the fish to a plate and leave to cool.
5 Remove any bones and cut the fish into 1 cm (½ in) pieces or flake it.
6 Add the cubed cucumbers and the capers to the fish.
7 Prepare the dressing by mixing together in a bowl the mayonnaise, brandy, lemon juice and ketchup until it is smooth.
8 To serve, arrange the fish mixture in champagne-type glasses and pour a little of the dressing over each.
9 Top it with a little ketchup and a slice of lemon.

GEHAKTE LEBER
Chopped liver

Chopped liver is traditionally eaten for lunch on Saturdays. It originated as a means of using the giblets of the Sabbath chicken and it makes a simple and cheap hors d'oeuvre that can be made on Friday and eaten on Saturday after the synagogue service.

Serve on a bed of lettuce leaves with matzo crackers, french bread or rolls and butter.

As well as chicken livers it is possible to make this dish using calf or ox liver.

50 g (2 oz) chicken fat (in non-kosher homes butter can be used instead)
450 g (1 lb) chicken livers, trimmed
1 large onion, very finely chopped
2 hard-boiled eggs, shelled and chopped
1 teaspoon salt
½ teaspoon black pepper

1 Melt the fat in a frying pan, add the chicken livers and fry them, turning occasionally, for about 5 minutes or until they are lightly browned.
2 Remove the livers with a slotted spoon and set aside.
3 Add the onion to the pan and fry, stirring occasionally, until soft but not brown.
4 Remove the pan from the heat.
5 Chop the livers finely and stir them into the onion together with the hard-boiled eggs, salt and pepper.
6 With a little fat, grease a small terrine or earthenware dish.
7 Spoon the liver mixture into the dish and lightly press it down.
8 Cover with foil and chill overnight.
9 To serve, turn the liver mould out of the dish and serve it either whole or sliced on a bed of lettuce leaves.

GEHAKTE HERRING
Chopped herring salad

'If you cannot afford chicken, herring will do.'

Herring has a particularly strong attraction to Ashkenazim Jews who have numerous recipes making use of this fish. A few famed dishes should be noted, eg 'Herring salad', 'Pickled herring with apples', 'Herring cooked in olive oil' and 'Herring baked in filo pastry' which is one of my favourites, but which sounds much nicer in Yiddish: 'Gehakte herring in bletterteig'.

Jews have a strong traditional love of fish. I am told by Turkish friends that in the past (and for all I know, even today) Jews would be seen walking in the streets of Istanbul eating small fish – like our traditional fish and chips and the American equivalents of Kentucky chicken or burgers. The Turkish Jews (mostly of Latino, ie

Spanish, origin) would keep their fish in their coat pockets – out of sight!

This is an Ashkenazim recipe popular throughout Israel since a large proportion of modern Israelis are of Polish and Russian extraction and this dish is one of the classics of the 'Pale of Settlement'.

The seasoning of chopped herring is a matter of family tradition and tastes. Some people prefer vinegar to lemon juice and crumbled biscuits to matzo meal. This typical recipe makes an excellent appetizer as well as a fine buffet dish when spread on biscuits.

    4 salt herrings
    2 hard-boiled eggs, peeled
    1 small apple, peeled and cored
    1 small onion, finely chopped
    1 tablespoon caster sugar
    2 tablespoons medium matzo meal or crumbled
        digestive biscuits
    4 tablespoons vinegar or 2–3 tablespoons of lemon juice
    ½ teaspoon white pepper

To serve:
Cos lettuce leaves

For garnish:
Small gherkins, green olives and sliced tomatoes

1 The day before you make the salad cut the heads off the herrings, slit the bellies and remove the entrails.
2 Wash thoroughly, place in a casserole, cover with water and leave until the next day.
3 Remove the herrings and drain thoroughly on kitchen paper.
4 With a sharp knife slit the skin down the centre back and peel off the skin on either side with your fingers.

5 Flatten the back of each herring with the palm of your hand, turn over and lift out the centre bone as well as any other bones.

6 Cut the fish up roughly on a large chopping board, add the eggs, apple and onion and continue chopping until all the ingredients are very fine. (A double-handled chopping knife is very good for this job.) Alternatively you could pass the ingredients through a mincer and squeeze out any excess liquid.

7 Place the chopped ingredients in a large bowl and add the vinegar or lemon juice, the matzo meal or biscuits and the sugar and white pepper.

8 Mix well and refrigerate for a few hours.

9 Serve on a large platter on a bed of lettuce leaves and garnished with the gherkins, olives and tomatoes.

DAG-MALOOLAH IM TAPOUZIM
Herrings with apples

'What is it that hangs on the wall, is green and whistles?'
'A herring.'
'A herring? Does a herring hang on a wall?'
'Who stops you from hanging it?'
'Is a herring green?'
'It could be painted green.'
'But whoever heard of a herring that whistles?'
'Nu! so it doesn't whistle!'

from the *Treasury of Jewish Quotations*

This is a delicious recipe combining herring with apples. Herring is a rich fish which is also very nutritious since 2 fish will provide an adult with his full daily requirement of protein.

This dish can be refrigerated for 2–3 days.

4 salt herrings
2 medium eating apples, peeled, cored and cubed

1 onion, finely chopped
1 pickled cucumber, diced

For the dressing:
75 g (3 oz) sugar
3 tablespoons oil
90 ml (3 fl oz) vinegar
½ teaspoon mixed mustard
3 tablespoons tomato purée
2 bay leaves
1 teaspoon salt
½ teaspoon white pepper

1 The day before you make the salad cut the heads off the herrings, slit the bellies and remove the entrails.
2 Wash thoroughly, place in a casserole dish, cover with water and leave until the next day.
3 Remove the herrings and drain thoroughly on kitchen paper.
4 With a sharp knife slit the skin down the centre back and peel off the skin on either side with your fingers.
5 Flatten the back of each herring with the palm of your hand, then turn it over and lift out the centre bone as well as any other bones.
6 Cut the fish into chunks.
7 Mix all the dressing ingredients together in a large bowl.
8 Add the chopped fish, apples, onion and cucumber and mix thoroughly.
9 Place in the refrigerator to chill and then serve with black bread or pita.

TABOULI
Cracked wheat salad

Classic Syrian salad which is very popular in Israel. It is a peasant dish of great antiquity, going back to the days of the Phoenicians. I am quite sure the ancient Israelites loved this salad as much as the modern Israelis do – at least I would like to think so.

Burghul, of course, was the staple diet of the Middle East before rice arrived via Persia over a thousand years ago.

75 g (3 oz) fine burghul
½ cucumber, finely chopped
4 tomatoes, finely chopped
1 green pepper, seeded and finely chopped
½ onion, finely chopped
4 tablespoons chopped parsley
2 tablespoons chopped dried mint
1½ teaspoons salt
juice of 2 lemons
4 tablespoons olive oil

To serve:
1 lettuce, preferrably Cos, washed

1 Rinse the burghul in a large bowl filled with cold water, several times.
2 Squeeze out any excess water.
3 Put all the chopped vegetables, parsley and mint into a large mixing bowl and add the burghul.
4 Stir in the salt, lemon juice and olive oil.
5 Mix well together, leave for 15 minutes and then taste and adjust seasoning if necessary.
6 Arrange the lettuce leaves around the edge of a serving plate and pile the salad into the centre.
7 To eat, make a parcel of the tabouli by folding a little of it up in a lettuce leaf or in the hollow of a pita bread.

Soups

Hymn

Meat and soup in the plate,
Knives and forks in a bunch.
Eat your food quickly,
Sing the song of munch.

Lettuce and tomatoes
Lots of juice contain.
A whole year of strength
Lies in one ear of grain.

Another lot of soup
In my plate pour,
Then to the kitchen
Go and make more . . .

Halper Leivick

Soups

MARAK ADASHIM	*Lentil soup*
	Middle Eastern lentil soup
	Jaffa lentil soup
MARAK HOBENE GROPEN	*Groat soup with meat*
SHELEG CHERMON	*Cold yogourt soup with nuts*
MARAK SHEZIF IM VE DUVDEVANIM	*Plum and cherry soup*
BORSHT	*Beetroot soup*
MILCHIK BORSHT	*Cold beetroot soup*
KHAMITZA IM MELATEFONIM	*Beetroot soup with cucumber*
MARAK AUFF	*Chicken soup*
MARAK AUFF IM RIMONIM	*Chicken soup with pomegranate*
MARAK BASAR	*Yemeni meat soup*
MARAK TARETIM	*Spinach and pine nut soup*
MARAK AVOCADO IM BATZAL	*Onion and avocado soup*
MANDLEN	*Soup noodles*

KNAIDLACH *Matzo balls*
MATZO LOKSHEN *Matzo noodles*

SOUPS

'Your neighbour's soup always smells good'

Proverb

When the first pioneers arrived in Palestine in the late
nineteenth century they were Polish- and Russian-speak-
ing folk who brought with them the food of Eastern
Europe, eg thick soups made with beetroot or cabbage
and potatoes – excellent fare for a cold climate but, as
time has shown, not suitable in warm, sub-tropical lands.

Today the soups of Israel are invariably lighter and
simpler, and although there are some people who retain
and hark back almost mystically to the customs and foods
of their grandparents from the 'Pale of Settlement' the
average Israeli (if there is such a person!) prefers simple,
locally produced vegetable-based soups. The choice is wide
yet there are certain distinguishable trends: (a) vegetables
and fruits are made much use of; (b) nuts and pulses figure
prominently; (c) traditional European soups such as borsht
and shchi are still popular; and (d) many indigenous Middle
Eastern soups of the Arabs, Turks, Yemenis etc have been
absorbed into the Jewish repertoire.

MARAK ADASHIM
Lentil soup

And Esau said to Jacob, Feed me, I pray thee, with that same
    red pottage; for I am faint . . .
And Jacob said, Sell me this day thy birthright.
And Esau said, Behold, I am at the point to die: and what profit
    shall this birthright do to me?
And Jacob said, Swear to me this day; and he sware unto him:
    and he sold his birthright unto Jacob.
Then Jacob gave Esau bread and pottage of lentiles; . . . thus
    Esau despised his birthright.

Genesis 25 (30–34)

This is one of the great soups of the Middle East, popular
with most Sephardim Jews and now with most Israelis.
There are several variations and I have included two. The
first is a general Middle Eastern one and the second is an
Israeli one from Jaffa. Any type of lentils will do and it is
not really necessary to soak them beforehand although it
does make shorter the cooking time.

Middle Eastern lentil soup
50 g (2 oz) margarine
1 onion, chopped
350 g (12 oz) lentils, washed
1 stick celery, chopped
1.8 litres (3 pints) water
2 marrow bones, cracked
2 teaspoons salt
1 teaspoon black pepper
1 teaspoon cumin

Garnish:
A little cumin and paprika
Fried croutons

1 Melt the margarine in a large saucepan, add the onion
  and sauté until soft.
2 Add the lentils, celery, water and bones.
3 Bring to the boil, lower the heat and simmer for about
  1 hour or until the lentils are very soft.
4 Season with the salt, pepper and cumin and simmer for
  a further 5 minutes.
5 Remove and discard the bones.
6 Rub the soup through a sieve and then reduce it to a
  purée in an electric blender.
7 Return the purée to the saucepan and add sufficient
  water to make it the consistency you prefer.
8 Bring just to the boil and adjust seasoning if necessary.

9 To serve, garnish with the cumin and paprika, adding a few croutons.

Jaffa lentil soup
½ tablespoon coriander leaves
3 cloves garlic
1 tablespoon cumin
1 teaspoon salt
4 tablespoons oil
275 g (9oz) lentils, washed
1.2 litres (2 pints) chicken stock
½ teaspoon black pepper
1 tablespoon flour mixed with 2 tablespoons water
2 spring onions, thinly sliced

To serve:
Juice of 1 lemon
2 tablespoons chopped parsley

1 In a small bowl mix together and then mash the coriander, garlic, cumin and salt.
2 Heat the oil in a large saucepan, add the spice mixture and sauté for 3–4 minutes.
3 Add the lentils, cover with boiling water and cook until the water evaporates and the lentils are tender. If necessary add a little more water while the lentils are cooking.
4 Drain the lentils and return to the saucepan.
5 Add the chicken stock and black pepper and bring quickly to the boil.
6 Add the flour-water mixture and stir until the soup thickens.
7 Stir in the spring onion slices.
8 Serve in individual bowls with a little lemon juice sprinkled in each and topped with some chopped parsley.

MARAK HOBENE GROPEN
Groat soup with meat

Hobene gropen is a variety of groats (hulled and crushed grain, usually oats, but sometimes wheat, barley or even maize). It is sold in most Jewish, Polish or East European shops and is popular throughout Israel.

This soup has a very distinctive flavour and is reputed to be very wholesome, due chiefly to its rich vitamin B content.

3 tablespoons hobene gropen
1.2 litres (2 pints) stock
110 g (¼ lb), or a little more, shin beef
1 teaspoon salt
¼ teaspoon white pepper
1 potato, cut into 1 cm (½ in) cubes
1 carrot, cut into ½ cm (¼ in) slices
1 onion, chopped
1 stick celery, cut into ½ cm (¼ in) slices
1 sprig parsley

For garnish:
2 tablespoons chopped parsley

1 Put the groats in a small pan, cover with boiling water and set aside.
2 Put the stock into a large saucepan and add the meat, salt and pepper and bring to the boil.
3 Drain the groats and add to the saucepan.
4 Reduce the heat, cover and simmer for 1 hour.
5 Add the vegetables and the sprig of parsley and continue simmering, covered, for about 1 hour until the meat is very tender.
6 Remove the sprig of parsley, taste and adjust the seasoning if necessary.

7 Serve immediately, sprinkled with the chopped
  parsley.

SHELEG CHERMON
Cold yogourt soup with nuts

This recipe is the creation of a well-known Israeli chef,
Arnold Barsysh, who was born in Rumania, lived in
Bulgaria and finally settled in Israel. This delightful soup
derives its inspiration from the rich yogourt-based dishes
of the Balkans, but it has a certain 'Israeliness' about it
with the use of nuts and mint.

  450g (1 lb) small cucumbers
  1 teaspoon salt
  1 teaspoon olive oil
  1 teaspoon dried dill
  6 cloves garlic, crushed
  900 ml (1½ pints) yogourt

  To serve:
  50 g (2 oz) walnuts and almonds, finely chopped
  4 sprigs fresh mint
  Ice cubes

1 Peel the cucumbers and cut into small cubes.
2 Season with the salt.
3 Add the olive oil, dill and garlic and mix well.
4 Add the yogourt and stir until the mixture is smooth
  and well blended. If you think it is too thick then add a
  little water until you have the consistency you prefer.
5 Refrigerate for a few hours.
6 Spoon the soup into individual bowls and place 2 ice
  cubes in each.
7 Sprinkle each bowl with the chopped nuts, decorate
  with a sprig of mint and serve immediately.

MARAK SHEZIF IM VE DUVDEVANIM
Plum and cherry soup

The Cherry Tree

You said:
Old, in pain,
a dry tree.
But for me there was
brilliant blossom
a breeze in the tree-top
the taste of your lips
on my lips –

don't be childish,
you said.
The dry tree will be firewood
now put the pot on the fire,
quick.

Originating from southern Russia, this soup makes a light and delicious first course for a summer meal. There are numerous variations and almost any fruit will do, eg apples, apricots, oranges, greengages etc.

It is traditionally served with smetana – soured cream – and garnished with fresh mint sprigs. If you prefer, yogourt makes an excellent substitute for the cream.

450 g (1 lb) plums, halved and stoned
225 g (½ lb) pears, peeled, halved, cored and thickly
    sliced
275 g (10 oz) cherries, halved and stoned
50g (2 oz) sugar
¼ teaspoon salt
1 teaspoon ground cinnamon
Juice and finely grated rind of 1 lemon
1.2 litres (2 pints) water
1 teaspoon cornflour

1 Place all the ingredients except the cornflour in a large saucepan and mix well. Bring to the boil, stirring occasionally. Lower the heat, cover the pan and simmer for 10–15 minutes or until the fruit is tender.

2 Remove from the heat and strain the contents of the pan through a sieve into a large bowl. Rub the fruit through with a wooden spoon and discard any pulp left in the sieve.

3 Return the soup to the pan.

4 In a small bowl mix the cornflour to a smooth paste with a few tablespoons of the soup.

5 Add the cornflour mixture to the soup, stirring constantly.

6 Slowly bring the soup back to the boil, stirring constantly. Lower the heat and simmer for a further 5 minutes or until the soup is smooth and has thickened slightly.

7 Taste and add more sugar if necessary. Set aside to cool.

8 Pour the soup into a serving bowl and refrigerate until ready to serve.

BORSHT
Beetroot soup

'For Borsht you don't need any teeth.'

Proverb

'Borsht' is the great soup of all the Russias. It is made of various ingredients in different combinations (I understand there are over 50 variations) but the main ingredient is the red beetroot.

The Jews of the 'Pale of Settlement', with the mass of the people of Russia, virtually lived on Borsht which, more often than not, had become the one and only meal of the day. Therefore a great deal of ingenuity was required on the part of housewives to vary and flavour the meal.

I have selected three Borshts which I found still popular in Israel, through the Polish, Russian and Ukrainian Jews who emigrated earlier this century and who have retained much of their traditional cuisine.

1 carrot, peeled and coarsely grated
1 small onion, thinly sliced
675 g (1½ lb) beetroot, peeled and coarsely grated
1.2 litres (2 pints) chicken stock
2 tablespoons sugar
2 teaspoons salt
¼ teaspoon white pepper
Juice of 1 lemon
2 eggs

1 Place all the vegetables in a large saucepan together with the stock, sugar, salt and pepper.
2 Bring slowly to the boil.
3 Lower the heat, cover and simmer for about 1 hour.
4 Pour the contents of the saucepan through a coarse sieve into a large bowl.
5 Discard the vegetables.
6 Return the liquid to the pan.
7 Beat the eggs in a small bowl.
8 Bring the soup to the boil then lower the heat and add the lemon juice.
9 Add a little of the beetroot soup to the eggs and mix in thoroughly.
10 Lower the heat under the soup to an absolute minimum then gradually stir in the egg mixture.
11 Cook for a further 10 minutes, but *do not boil* or the soup will curdle.
12 Serve immediately.

MILCHIK BORSHT
Cold beetroot soup

1 Use the ingredients as listed in the foregoing recipe, using water instead of stock.
2 When cooked, cool and then chill overnight.
3 Stir in some 'smetana' – soured cream.
4 Serve chilled.

KHAMITZA IM MELATEFONIM
Beetroot soup with cucumber

This is a Borsht which has acquired a touch of the Orient with the inclusion of cucumber and yogourt.

1 large beetroot, boiled, skinned and diced
½ cup of beet leaves, washed and chopped
600 ml (1 pint) yogourt
600 ml (1 pint) smetana (soured cream)
1 spring onion, finely chopped
½ teaspoon salt
¼ teaspoon black pepper
3 potatoes, peeled and thickly sliced
600 ml (1 pint) chicken stock
1 medium cucumber, coarsely chopped
3 hard-boiled eggs, sliced

1 In a large saucepan mix together the beetroot, beet-root leaves, yogourt, smetana, spring onion, salt and pepper.
2 Bring just to the boil and simmer for 3 minutes.
3 Remove from the heat, cool and then refrigerate for 3 hours.
4 In a large saucepan boil the potato slices in the chicken stock until just tender, drain and keep warm.
5 In a bowl cover the cucumber with boiling water and leave for 2–3 minutes.

6 Rinse the cucumber under cold water and drain.
7 Stir the cucumber and sliced eggs into the beetroot
  mixture.
8 Place the warm potato slices in the bottom of individual soup bowls.
9 Add the soup and serve immediately.

MARAK AUFF
Chicken soup

'When a miser becomes extravagant he eats chicken soup with
honey cake.'

Proverb

This is the soup of the 'Pale of Settlement'. No other
people have managed to master the art of cooking chicken
in quite the same way. The Jewish housewives have, over
the ages, created a cuisine where every part and parcel of
a chicken is used, including the heart, giblets, neck and
carcase.

This soup is traditionally made by simmering the
chicken, or parts of it, in water with vegetables. The flesh
is then used for other purposes, eg salad, dumplings etc,
and the flavour and substance of the soup is enriched with
the many 'noodles' cleverly devised by the housewives, eg
lokshen, knaidlach, mandlen etc (see recipes, pages
97–99).

1.8 litres (3 pints) water
1 chicken stock cube
450 g (1 lb) chicken flesh or 225 g (½ lb) chicken plus
    giblets
1 teaspoon salt
¼ teaspoon white pepper
1 onion, chopped
2 carrots, peeled and each cut into 8 pieces

2 sticks celery, leaves and the top 7.5 cm (3 in) only, chopped
1 sprig parsley
1 tomato, chopped

For garnish:
Lokshen, knaidlach, mandlen etc

1 Put the water, stock cube, chicken (and giblets), salt and pepper into a large saucepan and bring to the boil.
2 Remove any froth that appears on the surface.
3 Add the onion, carrot, celery, parsley and tomato.
4 Cover the pan and simmer for about 2 hours or until the chicken flesh is very tender.
5 Strain the soup through a sieve into a large bowl.
6 Remove the chicken flesh, giblets and carrots. Put the chicken flesh aside to use in another recipe. Reserve the giblets and carrots to add to the soup later.
7 Place the bowl of soup in the refrigerator.
8 When required remove the soup from the fridge and remove and discard the fat.
9 Reheat the soup, taste and adjust the seasoning if necessary.
10 Chop the giblets and carrots very finely and return them to the soup.
11 Cook for a further 5–10 minutes.
12 Serve hot with the garnishes of your choice.

MARAK AUFF IM RIMONIM
Chicken soup with pomegranates

'Who will help me pick the pomegranate and the honey-dew, the jasmine and the musk?'

'Song of Songs'

This is an Israeli soup making use of pomegranates and aubergines. An Israeli friend introduced this delicious dish to me and I took an instant liking to it.

I prefer to use a little concentrated pomegranate juice instead of fresh juice, but the former is very difficult to find in Europe. It is usually sold in a concentrated form in Syria and Lebanon and it *can* be found in a few specialist shops here. If you do manage to find some, use it sparingly as it is very concentrated.

1.2 litres (2 pints) water
450 g (1 lb) chicken flesh, diced
1 stick celery, cut into 1 cm (½ in) pieces
3 spring onions, cut into 2.5 cm (1 in) pieces
1 aubergine, peeled and cut into 1 cm (½ in) cubes
2 pomegranates
3 tablespoons sugar
1 teaspoon salt
Juice of 1 lime or large lemon

1 Pour the water into a large saucepan and bring to the boil.
2 Add the diced chicken, celery and spring onions and simmer for 5–7 minutes.
3 Add the pieces of aubergine and continue cooking for 15 more minutes.
4 Meanwhile halve the pomegranates and scoop out the seeds.
5 Blend the seeds in a liquidizer.
6 Strain the pulp and squeeze out as much juice as possible.
7 Add the pomegranate juice to the soup.
8 Stir in the sugar, salt and lime or lemon juice.
9 Lower the heat and simmer for a further 20 minutes.
10 Taste and adjust seasoning if necessary.
11 Serve immediately.

MARAK BASAR
Yemeni meat soup

According to some theories the 'real' Jews lived in the Yemen. They spoke a kind of Hebrew amongst themselves, intermarried and thus kept their ethnic purity. Almost all the Yemenite Jews returned to Israel in 1948 in what came to be known as 'Operation Magic Carpet'. They brought with them a touch of the exotic. Small, thin, dark people with piercing eyes and a deep devotion, the Yemenites soon settled in their new country and improved their lot. They are excellent goldsmiths and silversmiths, creating and re-creating intricate patterns first developed thousands of years ago in Southern Arabia.

Naturally the Yemenis also brought with them their food – spicy and hot. Unfortunately, but understandably, the younger generation are abandoning their traditional food for the simpler, international kind.

Yemenis use a spicy seasoning-cum-dip called Hawayij to enhance several of their dishes, one being this thick and filling soup which is really a meal in its own right.

450 g (1 lb) beef shoulder, cut into 1 cm (½ in) pieces after removing fat
2–3 marrow bones
6 whole cloves garlic, unpeeled
1 onion, coarsely chopped
1 carrot, peeled and cut into 1 cm (½ in) rounds
1 large tomato, quartered
4 sprigs parsley
4 sprigs dill, or 2 teaspoons dried dillweed
1 courgette, trimmed and cut into 1 cm (½ in) rounds
2 potatoes, peeled and cut into 1 cm (½ in) cubes
4 celery stalks, cut into 1 cm (½ in) pieces
1 teaspoon salt

Hawayij
1 tablespoon whole black peppercorns
1 tablespoon caraway seeds
1 teaspoon cardamon seeds
2 teaspoons turmeric

1 First prepare the Hawayij by placing the ingredients in
   a mortar and pounding to a powder. Store in a jar with
   a lid and use in this and other recipes.
2 Place the meat and marrow bones in a large saucepan
   with about 2.5 litres (4 pints) water and bring to the
   boil. Skim off every bit of the froth that appears on the
   surface. Add the garlic, onion, carrot, parsley and dill,
   lower the heat, cover the pan and simmer for 45
   minutes.
3 Remove the marrow bones and add the courgette,
   potatoes and celery and simmer for a further 20
   minutes.
4 Stir in the salt and 2–3 teaspoons of the prepared
   hawayij, depending on taste, and simmer for 10 minutes. Remove the garlic cloves.
5 Serve the soup just as it is, with bread, or place some
   cooked rice or noodles in the bottom of each soup
   bowl, spoon some of the meat and vegetables on top
   and then pour some of the liquid over them.

MARAK TARETIM
Spinach and pine nut soup

A lovely and flavoursome soup of spinach with nuts and
milk. The use of nutmeg is quite brilliant – increase the
proportion if you wish to emphasize the aroma of the
spice.

3 tablespoons butter
½ onion, finely chopped
50 g (2 oz) pine nuts

25 g (1 oz) chopped walnuts, or hazelnuts, or a mixture
   of the two
2 tablespoons flour
1.2 litres (2 pints) chicken stock
350 g (¾ lb) fresh spinach, washed thoroughly and
   then chopped
300 ml (½ pint) milk
Salt and pepper to taste
½ teaspoon ground nutmeg

1 Melt the butter in a large saucepan, add the onion and
  fry until soft and just turning golden.
2 Add the nuts and fry, stirring frequently until golden.
3 Sprinkle in the flour and mix thoroughly. Stir in the
  chicken stock and bring to the boil.
4 Add the spinach and simmer for about 5 minutes or
  until the spinach is tender.
5 Add the milk and return to the boil. Season with the
  salt, pepper and nutmeg. The amount of salt and
  pepper will depend on the degree of seasoning in the
  chicken stock.

MARAK AVOCADO IM BATZAL
Onion and avocado soup

Avocados have become – more than any other fruit – the
fruit of Israel. The Israeli chefs have devised countless
ways of using this fruit of West Indian origin, which is
shaped like a large pear and has a most distinctive flavour
and texture.

I like this soup very much although I must admit that I
needed to try quite a few avocados before I really began to
appreciate their peculiar taste. All (well, almost all!) my
Israeli friends rave about avocados and I am sure that it is
not mere chauvinism.

4 tablespoons oil
1 onion, chopped
2 spring onions, chopped
2 cloves garlic, crushed
1.2 litres (2 pints) chicken stock
Small pinch salt
½ teaspoon black pepper
¼ teaspoon nutmeg
1 ripe avocado, peeled and mashed
1 teaspoon lemon juice
Grated rind of 1 lemon
1 egg yolk

For garnish:
1 tablespoon finely chopped parsley

1 Heat the oil in a large saucepan, add the onion, spring onions and garlic and sauté for about 5 minutes, stirring frequently, until the onion is golden brown.
2 Add the stock, salt, pepper and nutmeg and bring to the boil.
3 Lower the heat and simmer for 30 minutes, stirring occasionally.
4 Mash the lemon juice and rind into the avocado and add it to the soup.
5 Mix well and simmer for a further 5 minutes.
6 Beat the egg yolk in a small bowl, add a few table-spoons of the soup and mix well.
7 Add the egg mixture to the soup, stir well and simmer for a further 5 minutes.
8 Taste and adjust seasoning if necessary.
9 Serve garnished with the chopped parsley.

MANDLEN
Soup noodles

'How just is the Lord. The rich he gives food – to the poor he gives appetite.'

Proverb

The Russians have 'lapsha', the Rumanians 'polenta', the Greeks, Turks and Armenians 'tarkhania' and the Jews have 'mandlen'. All are basically the same, ie small pieces of dough that are baked or fried and then added to soup to enrich it and to make a substantial meal. The principle is as old as society and the origins could possibly be Mongolian.

Mandlen can be cooked in advance and stored until needed. In a hot climate such as Turkey the dough is dried in the sun and then stored.

> 75 g (3 oz) plain flour
> ½ teaspoon salt
> 2 teaspoons vegetable oil
> 1 egg

1 Sift the flour and salt into a bowl.
2 Make a well in the centre and add the oil and egg.
3 Use your hands to mix to a soft dough.
4 Work the dough into a ball and divide into 2 or 3 portions.
5 Roll each portion out on a floured surface until thin.
6 Cut into long strips about 1 cm (½ in) wide and then cut them into 2.5 cm (1 in) lengths.
7 To bake: Arrange on flat greased baking sheets and place in an oven preheated to 190°C (375°F) Gas 5 to bake for 20 minutes or until golden brown. Remove from the oven, cool and store in airtight tins.
8 To fry: Leave the uncooked mandlen to stand for 30 minutes after being cut into shape. Heat some oil in a

frying pan and fry them, a few at a time, turning once, until they are golden brown.

Remove with a slotted spoon and drain on kitchen paper while the remainder are being cooked. When cold store in an airtight tin.

KNAIDLACH
Matzo balls

'It is not the Haggadah (narration of the Passover) that we like so much as the dumpling.'

Proverb

A traditional Central European speciality, knaidlach are also known as 'halkes' or 'matzo balls'. They are balls of matzo, onion, egg and spices which are cooked in the soup (they are ideal in chicken or tomato soup). In strict kosher houses knaidlachs are made with chicken or vegetable fat, but butter can be substituted. Sometimes ground almonds are used to enhance the flavour.

110 g (4 oz) matzo meal
120 ml (4 fl oz) boiling water
1 egg, lightly beaten
40 g (1½ oz) chicken or vegetable fat or butter
1 teaspoon salt
½ teaspoon white pepper
¼ teaspoon ground ginger
Pinch grated nutmeg
1 teaspoon chopped parsley

1 In a large bowl mix the matzo and water until well blended.
2 Add all the remaining ingredients and mix well for 4–5 minutes or until the mixture forms a soft dough.
3 Place the dough in the refrigerator for 1–1½ hours.

4 Remove and shape a little of the mixture into a small ball.
5 Test by dropping it into the boiling soup (or stew). If it falls apart then add a little more matzo to the mixture before forming the rest into small balls.
6 Drop the matzo balls carefully into the boiling soup (or stew) and simmer for 30 minutes.
7 Serve in the soup (or stew).

MATZO LOKSHEN
Matzo noodles

'A lot of singing and too few noodles.'

Proverb

These are 'noodles' similar to the Russian kletski, or knaidlach, or kleis etc. Basically they are thin, ½ cm (¼ in) strips of dough which are dropped into boiling soup and cooked for 5 minutes.

Matzo noodles are served traditionally during Passover.

4 eggs
4 tablespoons water
½ teaspoon salt
4 tablespoons matzo meal
25 g (1 oz) margarine

1 Break the eggs into a bowl, add the water and salt and beat with a fork.
2 Stir in the matzo meal.
3 Melt the margarine in a frying pan over low heat.
4 Pour about 2 tablespoons of the batter into the pan and tip and rotate the pan so that the batter covers the base.
5 Cook for 1–2 minutes, or until the crepe is lightly browned.

6 Turn onto a warmed plate and keep warm while you cook the remaining crepes.
7 Roll up each crepe and, with a sharp knife, cut it into strips.
8 Drop the strips into the boiling soup and cook for 3–5 minutes.
9 Serve hot.

Vegetable Dishes

Vegetable Dishes

KHAZILIM IM AGVANIOTH	*Aubergines with tomatoes*
BAMIA TEL-AVIV	*Okra Tel-Aviv style*
KISHUYIM MEVUSHALIM	*Pumpkin stew*
CHATZILIM MEVUSHALIM	*Aubergine casserole*
OUGAT YERAKOT MEMULAA	*Vegetable and rice pie*
OUGAT AGAS	*Cauliflower and pear pie*
KOUSA MAHSHI	*Sautéed courgettes*
GEZER VE TABOUKHETZ	*Carrot and apple casserole*
PITRIOT BE-SHAMENET	*Mushrooms with soured cream*
LOKSHEN KUGEL MIT KAYZ UN EPPEL	*Apple, cheese and noodle pudding*
KHAZILIM KUGEL	*Aubergine pudding*
KISHUIM KUGEL	*Courgette pudding*

VEGETABLE DISHES

'Whether you chew it or not – the main thing is to swallow it!'

Proverb

On a walk through the centuries-old narrow streets of Jerusalem, steeped in legend, history and multi-layers of past cultures, one is confronted with glimpses of today in the shape of TV sets, video equipment, bright enamelled fridges and the odd car that squeezes through cobbled passages darkened by time, use and misuse. Every now and then a small, cell-like shop appears, glowing with rows and rows of 'Holy Land souvenirs'. There was a time when only crosses and Islamic symbols were displayed, now the ever-versatile, capitalist-oriented bazaar merchants display the Star of David alongside portraits of the Madonna and Child and Christ on the Cross. Incense permeates the chiaroscuro alleyways and the darkness is interrupted by the brilliant, dazzling and 'natural' colours of the earth in the shape of fruits and vegetables literally scattered about in apparent abundance. It is a thrill for a Westerner, used to a health-conscious and order-motivated background, to walk casually through these shops. The goodness of the land is there to touch, to taste before purchasing and this goodness is fresh, abundant and of the finest quality. It is not therefore surprising that these very vegetables are put to such good use by the Israeli housewives. The cuisine – both Jewish and Arab – is particularly rich in vegetable-based dishes, a few of which are included in this chapter.

KHAZILIM IM AGVANIOTH
Aubergines with tomatoes

This is a simple vegetable dish which is ideal with all meat dishes. If you wish you can substitute courgettes for aubergines.

2 large aubergines
50 g (2 oz) flour
2 eggs
oil for frying
6 large tomatoes

1 Peel and slice the aubergines crossways into 1 cm (½ in) slices.
2 Spread the flour over a plate; beat the 2 eggs in a small bowl.
4 Coat each aubergine slice first with flour and then dip it into the beaten eggs.
3 Heat some oil in a frying pan.
5 Place a few of the coated aubergine slices in the pan and fry, turning once, until they are golden brown on both sides.
6 When they are cooked place them in a saucepan.
7 Cook the remaining slices in the same way, adding them to the saucepan. (It may be necessary to add a little more oil to the frying pan.)
8 Blanch and peel the tomatoes and chop them.
9 Place the chopped tomatoes over the aubergines in the saucepan.
10 Season the vegetables with salt and pepper.
11 Cover the pan and cook over a very low heat for about 1 hour.
12 Although usually eaten hot this dish is also very tasty served cold with pita bread.

BAMIA TEL-AVIV
Okra Tel-Aviv style

This recipe makes use of okra – ladies' fingers – in a simple stew. It is a typical mid-eastern-style vegetable dish which is ideal with kebabs or roast meat and a rice pilav.

2 tablespoons olive oil
1 small onion, finely chopped
2 cloves garlic, chopped
450 g (1 lb) okra (ladies' fingers)
1 small green pepper, seeded and thinly sliced
1 tomato, chopped
½ teaspoon black pepper
300 ml (½ pint) stock
1 teaspoon salt
2 tablespoons lemon juice

1 Heat the oil in a large saucepan and add the onion and garlic.
2 Sauté until the onion is golden brown.
3 Add the okra, green pepper, tomato and black pepper.
4 Pour in the stock and stir well.
5 Bring to the boil, cover, lower the heat and cook for 30 minutes, or until the okra is just tender. Do not overcook or the okra will become 'stringy'.
6 Stir in the salt and lemon juice during the last 3 minutes of cooking.
7 Serve immediately.

Serves 4

KISHUYIM MEVUSHALIM
Pumpkin stew

Pumpkins are abundant and relatively cheap in Israel. However, they are not, in my opinion, very well exploited. They are a wholesome vegetable and can be cooked in many different ways. Above all they make excellent stews, with or without meat, as well as exquisite sweets.

Serve this dish as an accompaniment to roast meats and
kebabs.

    1½ tablespoons butter
    1 small onion, finely chopped
    1 clove garlic, finely chopped
    150 ml (¼ pint) tomato juice
    Juice of 1 lemon
    1 teaspoon salt
    ½ teaspoon black pepper
    ½ teaspoon allspice
    900 g (2 lb) pumpkin, cut into 5 cm (2 in) pieces

For garnish:
1 teaspoon paprika pepper

1 Melt the butter in a large saucepan.
2 Add the onion and fry until soft.
3 Add the garlic, tomato juice, lemon juice, salt, black
   pepper and allspice and stir well.
4 Add the pumpkin pieces and stir gently until the
   mixture begins to boil.
5 Cover the pan, lower the heat and simmer for 30–45
   minutes, or until the pumpkin is soft and tender, but
   not mushy.
6 Pile into a serving dish and sprinkle with the paprika.

CHATZILIM MEVUSHALIM
Aubergine casserole

This recipe is an Israeli version of the Middle Eastern
'guvege' or 'turlu'. The European equivalent is perhaps
'ratatouille'. Ratatouille, of course, is simply a vegetable
stew.

I have included two recipes for aubergine casserole
which illustrate very well the Oriental and the Western
backgrounds of the modern Israeli cuisine. The first is of

the former while the second, with its introduction of mustard and fennel, has a more Western approach.

Oriental version
60 ml (2 fl oz) vegetable oil
2 aubergines, peeled and cut into 2.5 cm (1 in) pieces
2 large onions, coarsely chopped
2 green peppers, seeded and cut into 5 cm (2 in) pieces
5 tomatoes, blanched, peeled and quartered
1–2 heads celery, root end and leaves cut off and tough
    outer stalks removed
2 cloves garlic, finely chopped
3 bay leaves
1½ teaspoons salt
½ teaspoon black pepper
½ teaspoon turmeric

1 Heat the oil in a large casserole.
2 Add all the vegetables and mix well.
3 Add all the seasonings and mix until well blended.
4 Cover and cook over a low heat, stirring occasionally, for about 1 hour or until the vegetables are nice and tender.
5 Serve hot or cold as an accompaniment to any roast meat of your choice.

Western-style version
2 aubergines, cut into 1 cm (½ in) slices
3 tablespoons dry mustard
1 teaspoon salt
½ teaspoon black pepper
½ teaspoon cayenne pepper
50 g (2 oz) butter or margarine, melted
1 large onion, thinly sliced
2 large tomatoes, sliced

2 green peppers, seeded and cut into ½ cm (¼ in)
   slices
1 stalk fennel, diced
½ teaspoon allspice

1 Coat each aubergine slice lightly with the mustard and
   arrange them on a large plate.
2 Sprinkle the slices with the salt and black and cayenne
   pepper.
3 Grease a casserole with a little of the butter or
   margarine and arrange half the aubergine slices over
   the base.
4 Now arrange the onion, tomatoes, green peppers and
   fennel over the aubergine.
5 Top with the remaining aubergine slices and sprinkle
   with the allspice.
6 Dribble the remaining butter over the top then cover
   the casserole and bake in an oven preheated to 190°C
   (375°F) Gas 5 for about 1¼ hours or until the vegetables are tender.
7 Serve warm as an accompaniment to meat dishes.

OUGAT YERAKOT MEMULAA
Vegetable and rice pie

This makes a substantial meal in itself, but I think it also
makes an excellent accompaniment to kebabs or roast
meat.
   I feel there is a touch of the USA about this dish though
I cannot be sure since it is widely popular throughout
Israel, so it may well be an indigenous recipe.

25 g (1 oz) butter
1 green pepper, seeded and thinly sliced
110 g (4 oz) cooked rice

1 tin sweet corn, or 2–3 fresh corn cobs with the
  kernels removed with a sharp knife
225 g (8 oz) peas
2 carrots, peeled and thinly sliced
2 eggs, separated
1 teaspoon salt
½ teaspoon black pepper
½ teaspoon thyme
2 tablespoons finely chopped parsley
2 tablespoons sultanas
250 ml (8 fl oz) chicken stock
3–4 tablespoons breadcrumbs
1 tablespoon made-up mustard

1 Heat the butter in a large saucepan and sauté the green
  pepper until soft.
2 Turn the green pepper into a large bowl and mix in the
  rice, sweetcorn, peas and carrots.
3 Stir in the egg yolks and add the salt, black pepper,
  thyme, parsley and sultanas.
4 Add the chicken stock and mix thoroughly.
5 Lightly grease a baking dish.
6 Sprinkle half the breadcrumbs over the base and stir
  the remainder into the vegetable mixture.
7 Pile the mixture into the dish, smooth over and place
  in an oven preheated to 180°C (350°F) Gas 4.
8 Cook for 25 minutes.
9 Meanwhile whisk the egg whites until stiff, add the
  mustard and mix well.
10 At the end of the 25 minutes remove the dish from the
  oven and spread the egg and mustard mixture over the
  top.
11 Return to the oven and cook for a further 15 minutes
  or until the crust is golden.
12 Serve immediately.

OUGAT AGAS
Cauliflower and pear pie

Cauliflowers with pears! Yes, they do in fact go well together as this recipe indicates. The dish makes an excellent accompaniment to any roast meat, particularly venison, chicken or turkey.

1 large cauliflower
3 unripe pears, peeled, cored and sliced
4 eggs, beaten
1 teaspoon salt
½ teaspoon black pepper
½ teaspoon nutmeg
4 tablespoons breadcrumbs
2 red peppers, seeded and cut into 1 cm (½ in) slices
6 black olives, stoned and sliced
6 mushroom caps, washed and thinly sliced
2 tablespoons finely chopped onion

For garnish:
1 tablespoon finely chopped parsley

1 Remove any leaves and break the cauliflower into florets. Wash thoroughly.
2 Drop the florets into a large pan of boiling water.
3 After 10 minutes add the pears and cook until tender.
4 Drain and cool slightly, then put the cauliflower, pears, eggs, salt, pepper, nutmeg and breadcrumbs into a liquidizer and blend.
5 Lightly grease a baking dish large enough to hold the mixture.
6 Pour about a quarter of the cauliflower mixture into the dish.
7 Cover with half each of the red pepper and olive slices.
8 Now pour in another quarter of the cauliflower mixture and cover it with the mushrooms and onions.

9 Add another cauliflower layer followed by the remaining red pepper and olive slices.

10 Top with the remaining cauliflower.

11 Place in an oven preheated to 180°C (350°F) Gas 4 and bake for 30–45 minutes or until the top is golden.

12 Sprinkle with the parsley and serve.

KOUSA MAHSHI
Sautéed courgettes

An Arab recipe, but popular with all Israelis. The Hebrew title is Kishuyim Metugarim.

The dish makes a fine accompaniment to meat, fish or poultry. It is usually eaten warm, but can be served cold as a salad on a buffet table or as part of a 'mezzeh' (Arabic for hors d'oeuvre).

> 60 ml (2 fl oz) olive oil
> 2 large onions, coarsely chopped
> 1 clove garlic, crushed
> 675 g (1½ lb) courgettes, topped and tailed
> 1 teaspoon salt
> ¼ teaspoon chilli pepper
> 1 tablespoon chopped fresh basil, or 1 teaspoon dried basil
> Juice of 1 lemon

1 Heat the oil in a large pan, add the onion and garlic and sauté until the onion is soft.

2 Chop the courgettes coarsely and add to the pan. Add the remaining ingredients and mix well.

3 Cook over a medium heat for about 15 minutes, stirring frequently, until the vegetables are just tender. Do not overcook.

4 Serve hot or cold.

GEZER VE TABOUKHETZ
Carrot and apple casserole

'Only in dreams are carrots as big as bears'

Proverb

A favourite from Central Europe which is now the speciality of most good Israeli hotels and restaurants. 'Gebakene mayeren un eppel tzimmes' – to give it its Yiddish name – makes a fine accompaniment to all cuts of meat.

Next time you are roasting a chicken try this vegetable casserole as an accompaniment, together with roast potatoes.

> 6 medium carrots, peeled and cut into ½cm (¼ in) rounds
> 4 medium cooking apples, peeled, cored and sliced
> ½ teaspoon salt
>
> *For the topping:*
> 2 tablespoons melted chicken fat or margarine
> 25g (1 oz) brown sugar
> ½ teaspoon cinnamon
> pinch of nutmeg
> ½ teaspoon salt
> ¼ teaspoon black pepper

1 Place the carrots in a large saucepan, cover with water and bring to the boil. Lower the heat and simmer for 15 minutes.
2 Add the apple slices and salt and simmer for a further 5 minutes. Drain.
3 Generously grease a large ovenproof casserole and spread the carrot and apple slices out evenly in it.
4 Mix the topping ingredients together in a bowl and sprinkle evenly over the carrots and apples. Cover the

casserole and bake in an oven preheated to 180°C
(350°F) Gas 4 for 30 minutes. Remove the cover and
bake for a further 15 minutes or until the crust is
golden.

PITRIOT BE-SHAMENET
Mushrooms with soured cream

Some years ago, while on holiday in Moscow, I was served
this vegetable dish on three successive occasions in three
different restaurants. I deduced from this that the Russians have nothing but mushrooms and smetana.
Mushrooms are, perhaps, the most beloved vegetable of
the Slavs from Czechoslovakia to the Urals and beyond,
the autumn mushroom picking being a national tradition.
But mushrooms in the Middle East? Now that was a new
experience. Yet I was served this same dish in an expensive restaurant in Tel-Aviv. It now transpires that immediately the Jews of Russia, Poland, the Ukraine and the
other Slav lands arrived in Palestine they started growing
mushrooms in the dark of their rooms where, I gather, the
finest mushrooms can be cultivated. And there were many
such dark places in Palestine!

Smetana (soured cream) is fine, but I prefer yogourt
(see pages 132–135 for further details of these two dairy
products).

Serve with any main dish of your choice.

2 tablespoons butter
1 small onion, finely chopped
450 g (1 lb) mushrooms, wiped clean and thinly sliced
1 teaspoon salt
½ teaspoon black pepper
2 teaspoons flour
300 ml (½ pint) soured cream – warmed through (but
  do not boil or it will curdle)

1 Melt the butter in a large pan, add the onion and sauté until soft. Add the mushrooms and sauté for 2–3 minutes. Season with the salt and pepper.
2 Sprinkle the flour into the pan, stir well, cover the pan and cook over a low heat for 5 minutes.
3 Remove from the heat and gradually stir in the warmed cream. Serve immediately.

Serves 4

KUGEL

'If you eat kugel on the Sabbath you'll be full the whole week'

Jewish expression

Kugel is the Yiddish word for a kind of pudding which is not always sweet (see 'Lokshen Kugel' below), but usually savoury and made, for instance, with potatoes, courgettes, noodles, spaghetti etc. The origin of the name 'kugel' is covered with all kinds of suppositions and since one is dealing with a 'Jewish' theme it invariably has certain religious connotations. Thus, according to some, kugel is a reminder of the manna that the Children of Israel ate in their wanderings. Others claim that the Hebrew word kugel (meaning 'like a disc') is the source of the name because it resembles the shape of the manna in its roundness.

I have selected a few kugel since I regard this particular dish, with its variations, to be typically 'Jewish' – as against dishes of Central European, Arab or North African origin. The first recipe is for an apple, cheese and noodle kugel. I am using its true Yiddish name since this and similar dishes are popular with Ashkenazim Jews and particularly the ultra-orthodox Hassidim who live in the Mea Shearim district of Jerusalem as well as old Yaffo and in the Jewish Quarter of the Old City itself.

LOKSHEN KUGEL MIT KAYZ UN EPPEL
Apple, cheese and noodle pudding

450 g (1 lb) broad noodles
4 tablespoons melted butter or margarine
4 eggs, lightly beaten
50 g (2 oz) sugar
225 g (½ lb) cream cheese
225 g (½ lb) cottage cheese
300 ml (½ pint) soured cream
450 g (1 lb) green apples, peeled, cored and chopped
50 g (2 oz) raisins.

1 Half fill a large saucepan with lightly salted water and bring to the boil. Add the noodles and cook until tender, but firm. Drain.
2 Place the noodles in a large mixing bowl, pour over the melted fat and toss until all the noodles are coated.
3 Add all the remaining ingredients and mix well.
4 Butter a large, ovenproof dish and add the noodle mixture.
5 Bake in an oven preheated to 180°C (350°F) Gas 4 for about 1 hour or until golden.

The second recipe is for an aubergine kugel. This is a Mediterranean variation of great charm and well worth trying.

KHAZILIM KUGEL
Aubergine pudding

1 large aubergine, peeled and sliced
4 tablespoons melted butter or margarine
1 onion, finely chopped
1 green pepper, finely chopped
2 eggs
1 teaspoon salt

½ teaspoon black pepper
110 g (4 oz) medium matzo meal, or crushed cream
    cracker crumbs
50 g (2 oz) butter or margarine, melted
1 teaspoon paprika

1 Half fill a saucepan with lightly salted water and bring
   to the boil. Add the aubergine slices and simmer for
   15–20 minutes or until tender. Drain, place the slices
   in a bowl and mash to a purée. Leave to cool.
2 Heat the 4 tablespoons melted fat in a small pan, add
   the onion and green pepper and fry until soft. Add this
   mixture to the aubergine.
3 Add the eggs, salt and pepper and mix well. Stir in the
   matzo meal or crumbs.
4 Turn the mixture into a well greased casserole and
   smooth over the surface.
5 Pour the 50 g (2 oz) melted fat over the top and
   sprinkle with the paprika.
6 Bake in an oven preheated to 180°C (350°F) Gas 4 for
   about 45 minutes or until the top is golden and the
   sides crusty.

Here is a courgette kugel which is excellent as an accompaniment to meat and poultry dishes.

KISHUIM KUGEL
Courgette pudding

3 tablespoons oil or melted butter
1 medium onion, finely chopped
450 g (1 lb) courgettes, peeled, finely chopped or
    grated and placed in a sieve to drain
2 teaspoons sugar
½ teaspoon salt
1 teaspoon cinnamon

50 g (2 oz) raisins
25 g (1 oz) chopped walnuts
4 eggs, lightly beaten

1 Heat the oil or butter in a small pan, add the onion and sauté until golden.
2 Turn the contents of the pan into a large bowl and add all the remaining ingredients. Mix well.
3 Grease an ovenproof dish, add the courgette mixture and smooth over the surface.
4 Bake in an oven preheated to 200°C (400°F) Gas 6 for about 25 minutes or until set and lightly browned.

Egg and Dairy Dishes

Egg and Dairy Dishes

BETZA SABRA	*Egg sabra*
BETZIM TEMANIYOT	*Yemenite eggs*
EGGAH-BI-KORRAT	*Leek omelette*
PRASI-FUÇI	*Sephardi omelette*
BETZIM MALKHUTIOT	*Royal eggs*
PETRUSHKA OMELET	*Parsley omelette*
BLINTZ IM GVINA	*Cheese pancakes*
SMETANA AND YOGOURT	*Soured cream and yogourt*
LABNA	*Drained yogourt*
KADOUREY YOGOURT	*Yogourt balls*
ITRIOYT IM YOGOURT	*Noodles with yogourt*
BETZIM IM SMETANA	*Eggs in soured cream*

EGG AND DAIRY DISHES

'Young hens lay eggs – old cows give milk'

Proverb

In place of a brief introduction here is a little story with a moral. One day Rabbi Jacob Krantz was visiting a rich man's house to collect alms for the needy. The host was famed for his avarice. The Rabbi told him about the generosity of his neighbours.

'They aren't that rich so they give a little now and then. Now I, on the other hand, have bequeathed my all to charity – after my demise, naturally.'

'Naturally,' said the Rabbi. 'Let me tell you a parable. There are two kinds of animals in the world. The hen that lays an egg at a time and the pig that gives fat and meat. How people love the hen, but dislike the pig. Do you know why, my son?'

'No.'

'Because the hen gives a little every day when it is needed, whilst the pig gives a great deal – only when it's dead.'

Jews in general and Israelis in particular have a rich repertoire of dairy dishes. On the kibbutz the basic diet is dairy produce and vegetables. Over recent years some new and interesting dishes have been created in the said same kibbutzim. One such recipe is called Betza Sabra. Sabra is the name given to the Jews born in the State of Israel. It is the Arabic word for a species of cactus indigenous to the region – it is sweet and soft inside, hard and prickly outside.

BETZA SABRA
Egg sabra

'The egg of today is better than the hen of tomorrow'

Proverb

A little patience and care is needed in the preparation of these stuffed and fried eggs, but the effort is well worth it.

    4 eggs, hard boiled
    2 tablespoons 'tahina tarator' (see chapter on Sauces)
    1 egg, well beaten
    ½ teaspoon Worcestershire sauce
    4–5 cream cracker biscuits, crushed very finely
    Oil for frying

For serving:
4 lettuce leaves

For garnish:
Black olives
Tomato slices
Gherkins
½ teaspoon paprika

1 Cut the eggs in half lengthways.
2 Remove the yolks.
3 In a small bowl mash the yolks with the tahina tarator.
4 Divide this mixture into four and put a portion between each pair of egg whites.
5 Reshape into 4 whole eggs.
6 In a small bowl mix the beaten egg with the Worcestershire sauce.
7 Carefully dip the stuffed eggs into the egg-sauce mixture.
8 Roll each egg in the biscuit crumbs until covered generously.

9 In a small saucepan heat the oil.
10 Place the eggs very gently in the pan, two at a time, and deep-fry until golden brown.
11 Serve on individual plates, each egg bedded on a lettuce leaf.
12 Garnish with the olives, tomato slices, and gherkins and sprinkle with a little paprika.

Serves 4

BETZIM TEMANIYOT
Yemenite eggs

This is a Yemenite recipe for scrambled eggs and potatoes.

Yemenite food has attracted a great deal of attention in Israel. The Jews, who were the remnants of the once 'Jewish Kingdom' of Yemen, took their native dishes with them when they emigrated to Israel.

The success of this cuisine is due mainly to its clever use of spices – local as well as those adopted from the Indian subcontinent.

50 g (2 oz) margarine
1 onion, finely chopped
3 cloves garlic, finely chopped
4 eggs
3 stalks fennel, chopped
3 boiled potatoes, peeled and diced
3 large tomatoes, blanched, peeled and mashed with
   the back of a fork
¼ teaspoon each of black pepper, cayenne pepper,
   cumin and ginger
Pinch ground cloves
Pinch cinnamon
150 ml (¼ pint) water

1 Melt the margarine in a large saucepan or frying pan.
2 Add the onion and garlic and sauté until soft and golden brown.
3 Now add the eggs and scramble lightly.
4 Add all the remaining ingredients and cook over a low heat, stirring constantly, for about 10 minutes.
5 Serve immediately.

EGGAH-BI-KORRAT
Leek omelette

'Eggah' is an omelette of Persian origin where it is called 'kuku'. In reality eggah is more than an omelette. In the French-Spanish cuisine an omelette is predominantely eggs with a flavouring of ingredients of your choice. In the Middle East eggah is ingredients of your choice plus sufficient eggs to act as a binding agent.

Eggah is thick, can be eaten hot or cold, and can be prepared with almost any ingredients, eg meat, chicken, vegetables etc.

This recipe is particularly popular with the Palestinians who produce some of the finest leeks of the region.

675 g (1½ lb) leeks
50 g (2 oz) butter
1 tablespoon lemon juice
1 teaspoon salt
½ teaspoon black pepper
½ teaspoon allspice
6 eggs

1 Trim the roots off the leeks, cut off the rough tops of the leaves and remove any coarse outer leaves.
2 Wash the leeks carefully.
3 Cut the leeks into thin slices, place in a colander and rinse again.
4 In a large frying pan or saucepan melt the butter.

5 Add the leeks and sauté for 3–4 minutes.
6 Add the lemon juice, salt, pepper and allspice, lower the heat and simmer for 10–12 minutes or more until the leeks are tender.
7 Beat the eggs in a large bowl.
8 Add the leek mixture to the eggs and mix well.
9 Pour the mixture back into the pan and cook over a very low heat until the eggs are set.
10 Cut into segments and serve with a fresh salad.

PRASI-FUÇI
Sephardi omelette

'Eggs want to be smarter than hens'

Proverb

This is simply an omelette, undoubtedly of Spanish origin, in the same tradition as the Arab 'eggah' or the Persian 'kuku'. I am sure the Arabs took it from the Persians, passed it on to the Spanish who then introduced it to the Jews who have now reintroduced it (albeit with slight modifications) into the Middle Eastern cuisine. Although usually served hot it can also be eaten cold and thus makes an excellent buffet dish. It can also be cut into 1 cm (½ in) squares, put on cocktail sticks and served as a 'nibble'.

25 g (1 oz) butter
1 small onion, chopped
110 g (4 oz) mushrooms, wiped clean and sliced
4 eggs
4 tablespoons milk
110 g (4 oz) fresh or thawed frozen spinach, chopped coarsely
150 g (5 oz) grated cheese eg Cheddar or Leicester
1 teaspoon salt
½ teaspoon black pepper
1 tablespoon finely chopped parsley

1 Heat the butter in a large frying pan and sauté the onion until golden brown.
2 Add the sliced mushrooms and cook for 3 minutes.
3 Meanwhile beat the eggs and milk together in a large bowl.
4 Add to the eggs the spinach, cheese, salt, pepper, parsley and the onion-mushroom mixture.
5 Turn this mixture into a lightly buttered casserole dish.
6 Place in an oven preheated to 190°C (375°F) Gas 5 and cook for about 30 minutes or until set and golden.

Serves 4

BETZIM MALKHUTIOT
Royal eggs

A regal dish, expensive both in cost and appearance. If you are fortunate enough to be able to afford caviar use Russian beluga or sevruga. Otherwise try 'imitation' caviar (Israeli, Danish or Norwegian). The dish makes a magnificent hors d'oeuvre.

    4 hard-boiled eggs
    300 ml (½ pint) beetroot juice
    225 g (½ lb) red cabbage, thinly shredded
    16 artichoke hearts, cooked until tender and drained
    4 tablespoons black caviar

Salsa malakh – Palace dressing:
    3 tablespoons mayonnaise
    3 tablespoons olive oil
    2 tablespoons vinegar
    2 spring onions, finely chopped

1 Shell the eggs and set them aside to soak in the beetroot juice until they are coloured purple.
2 On a large serving platter or small individual plates

arrange the shredded cabbage as though making small nests.

3 Cut each artichoke heart in quarters and place 8 quarters in each nest.
4 Cut each egg in half lengthways and place one half, cut side down, in the centre of each nest.
5 Mix the dressing ingredients together and season with extra salt and a little tabasco if necessary.
6 Cover each nest with some of the dressing and garnish with the caviar.
7 Serve any remaining dressing separately.

Serves 8

PETRUSHKA OMELET
Parsley omelette

From Russia with love, a simple, popular omelette. In Israel it is sold under the name 'Khavitat Petrozilia', but I prefer the sound of Petrushka.

8 eggs
6 tablespoons finely chopped parsley
2 tablespoons water
1 teaspoon salt
¼ teaspoon black pepper
2 tablespoons butter or margarine

1 Break the eggs into a large bowl. Add the parsley, water, salt and pepper and mix well.
2 Melt the fat in a large frying pan and swirl it around the base and sides.
3 Pour in the egg mixture, cover the pan and cook over a low heat for about 5 minutes or until set.

Serves 4

BLINTZ IM GVINA
Cheese pancakes

These savoury pancakes are delicious served with grilled or roast meat and/or salad.

> 350 g (¾ lb) grated cheese (a mixture of feta, Cheddar and cottage cheese is very successful, but you can experiment with whatever you have available)
> 2 eggs
> 1 tablespoon grated onion
> 2 tablespoons finely chopped parsley
> ½ teaspoon black pepper
> ¼ teaspoon allspice
> ½ teaspoon paprika
> A few tablespoons matzo meal
> Oil for frying

1 Put the cheese in a large bowl and thoroughly blend.
2 Break the eggs into the cheese, add the onion, parsley and spices and mix thoroughly.
3 Divide the mixture into 8 portions and mould, with your hands, into flat round pancakes.
4 Spread the matzo meal on a large plate and thoroughly coat each pancake on both sides.
5 Heat the oil in a large frying pan and then fry the pancakes gently until well cooked and golden on both sides.
6 Serve immediately.

Makes 8

SMETANA AND YOGOURT

It was once observed that Lemach's face became as though illuminated, and his brother philosophers realized that he had made a new discovery.

'What is it? What is it?' they asked.

'Thank heaven!' he answered. 'From now on every poor man will eat cream and every rich man drink sour milk. I've discovered how to do it. It is very simple!' he continued solemnly as they crowded around him. 'Let a decree be issued in Chelem that from now on sour milk shall be called cream and cream sour milk!'

SMETANA

This is also often known as soured cream and is of Eastern European origin – particularly popular in Poland, the Ukraine and Russia. Smetana is the skimmed off milk curds before they are put to drain for cheese.

Once, of course, smetana was made at home but today it is commercially produced by a method in which the cream is 'set', very much like yogourt, with a lactic acid bacillus. Soured cream keeps well in the refrigerator and can be substituted for fresh cream.

Most Israeli dishes of East European origin make great use of smetana in soups, stews and sweets. Mixed with fresh cream it has a distinctive flavour which goes particularly well with fresh fruit and sweet dessert dishes.

YOGOURT

Yogourt is of Middle Eastern origin and is particularly popular in Iran, Armenia, Turkey, Syria and Lebanon. Although unknown to most Ashkenazim Jews, yogourt and yogourt-based dishes have been eaten by Oriental Jews for generations and particularly by those Jews who originated from Middle Eastern lands.

Today yogourt is very popular in Israel, not only with Oriental Jews and the native Palestinian Arabs, but with a vast number of Israelis who have adopted this wholesome food and have integrated it into their new cuisine.

Yogourt can be bought commercially in its natural form as well as with added ingredients such as strawberries, peaches, bananas etc. However, I am a great advocate of all things natural and I recommend you to make your own yogourt for a better flavour as well as for economic reasons. There are several methods of making yogourt, but the one given below is the simplest and most proven.

1.2 litres (2 pints) milk
1 tablespoon 'live' yogourt or 'starter' (this can be bought in most foodstores, or use some from the batch of yogourt made previously)

1 Bring the milk to the boil in a large saucepan.
2 As the froth rises turn off the heat.
3 Allow the milk to cool to the point where you can dip in your finger and count to 15.
4 Put the tablespoon of yogourt (starter) into a teacup, add to it 3–4 tablespoons of the warm milk and mix well.
5 Pour this mixture into the milk and stir well.
6 Pour the milk–yogourt mixture into a bowl, place a plate over the top and then wrap the bowl in a teatowel.
7 Place the bowl in a warm place and leave without disturbing for about 8 hours or overnight.
8 Transfer the bowl to the refrigerator.

Yogourt will keep for up to a week before it goes sour. When you have almost used it up, save a little to use as a starter to make a fresh bowlful.

LABNA
Drained yogourt

Labna is a classic Middle Eastern appetizer, marvellous when eaten with warm pita. It is a must on any Syrian, Lebanese, Palestinian and, nowadays, Israeli breakfast

table. I found it served throughout the villages and
kibbutzes I visited.

The basic preparation is:

1 make the yogourt;
2 make a bag of muslin or fine cotton and pour the
  yogourt into this bag;
3 hang the bag for 10–12 hours or overnight so that the
  whey is drained off (this leaves a light, soft, creamy
  cheese – labna).
4 To serve, spread a few tablespoons over individual
  plates. Sprinkle with a few drops of olive oil and a little
  dried mint and decorate with a few black olives.

KADOUREY YOGOURT
Yogourt balls

1 Instead of hanging the yogourt for 10–12 hours or
  overnight, as in the previous recipe, hang it for at least
  2 days – this will further dry the yogourt.
2 Take down the bag and, with a spoon, remove the
  thickened labna and shape it into small walnut-sized
  balls.
3 Store these balls in a large glass jar half filled with olive
  oil and flavoured with 2 teaspoons cinnamon, 1 teaspoon cloves and a few sprigs of fresh mint leaves.
4 Close the jar tightly to make it airtight and store.
5 When required remove a few of the yogourt balls,
  arrange on a plate, garnish with a little paprika and a
  few black olives and serve for breakfast with bread.

ITRIOYT IM YOGOURT
Noodles with yogourt

This is another Israeli adaptation of what was once a
Persian dish. A local touch is the inclusion of ground
cumin – almost unknown in Iran.

This is one of my favourite dishes. It is nourishing and
health-giving and as well as being an ideal accompaniment for roast meats I like it as a quick snack with fresh
vegetables and some pita bread.

50 g (2 oz) fresh kidney beans, sliced
110 g (4 oz) thin noodles
2 tablespoons oil
½ onion, finely chopped
2 spring onions, thinly sliced
2 tablespoons raisins
3 tablespoons water
150 ml (¼ pint) yogourt
1 clove garlic, crushed
1 teaspoon salt
½ teaspoon black pepper
½ teaspoon ground cumin

1 In a small saucepan cook the kidney beans until
   tender in lightly salted boiling water.
2 Drain and set aside.
3 Bring a large saucepan of lightly salted water to the
   boil, add the noodles and simmer until they are
   tender.
4 Meanwhile heat the oil in a small saucepan, add the
   chopped onion and sauté until golden brown.
5 Add the spring onions and raisins and sauté for a
   further 2 minutes.
6 Add the water and simmer for about 5 minutes and
   then drain off any moisture which is left.
7 Stir in the cooked kidney beans.

8 When the noodles are cooked drain them into a colander and then transfer to a large serving bowl.
9 Mix the crushed garlic into the yogourt and stir through the noodles.
10 Season with the salt and pepper.
11 Stir the onion-bean mixture through the noodles and sprinkle with the cumin.
12 Either serve hot or chill for an hour or two and serve cold.

BETZIM IM SMETANA
Eggs in soured cream

Makes a fine breakfast, brunch or lunch when served with bread and perhaps a salad.

450 ml (¾ pint) soured cream
50 g (2 oz) dry breadcrumbs
25 g (1 oz) butter, melted
6 eggs
Salt and white pepper
50 g (2 oz) grated hard cheese, eg Cheddar

1 Pour half the cream into a shallow, ovenproof dish and then sprinkle with half the breadcrumbs and half the butter.
2 Carefully break the eggs, one at a time, into a small bowl and slide each one into the dish so that they are arranged evenly over the cream in one layer.
3 Sprinkle with salt and pepper to taste.
4 Cover evenly with remaining cream, crumbs and butter.
5 Sprinkle the cheese over the top.
6 Bake in an oven preheated to 170°C (325°F) Gas 3 for about 20 minutes or until the eggs are set.

Main Dishes

Main Dishes

MAIN DISHES

SINEA	*Baked minced meat*
SINEA CEM TAHINA	*Baked minced meat with tahina*
FILET BAKAR DRUCKER	*Beef fillet with liver*
TSLAOT EGAL NUSACH TSAYADIM	*Veal cutlets with mushroom sauce*
KEBAB NUSACH ISRAEL	*Israeli kebab*
BASAGH IM BANANAVE TMARIN	*Beef stuffed with bananas and dates*
BASAGH KEVIN IM RIMONIM	*Lamb with pomegranate*
BASAGH IM KOHLRABI	*Kohlrabi stuffed with avocado*
BASAGH EGAL IM MISHMISH	*Veal with apricots*
SHASHLIK	*Kidney and liver kebab*
DLA'AT MEMULET	*Pumpkin stuffed with lamb*
GOULASH TSOANI	*Gipsy-style goulash*
UMTZAT MASADA	*Beef fillet in puff pastry*
HOLISHKES	*Stuffed cabbage leaves*
CHOLENT	*Shabbat stew*
CHOLENT IM PEROT	*Cholent with fruit*
KIRSHEH	*Intestines stew*
KAHAL	*Spicy udder*

KOR'EE	*Shin with hawayij sauce*
GEED	*Penis stew*
LOCUST À LA YEMEN	*Dried locusts*
KEBAB ME AUFF	*Chicken kebab*
GEFILTE HELZEL	*Stuffed neck*
JEDJAD IMER	*Honeyed chicken*
AUFF MEMULAH NUSACH VIP	*Chicken VIP*
AUFF TEMANI	*Yemenite chicken*
GALIL CHAZEH HODU 'MERCHAVIA'	*Turkey breasts stuffed with minced meat*
AUFF MEMULAH IM KASHA	*Chicken stuffed with kasha*
OUGAT AUFF IM TAHINA	*Chicken pie*
MUKULI	*Chicken with lemon and olives*
CARPION MEMULA IM GVINAVE PITRINOT	*Carp stuffed with cheese and mushrooms*
DAG ISRAELI	*Israeli cod*
DAG BE TAHINA	*Fish with tahina*
DAG BE TAHINA BE EGOZIM	*Fish with tahina and nuts*
DAG-YAM-KINNERET	*St Peter's fish*
DAG IM BANAVOT	*Fish with bananas*
DAG METUGAN NO SAKHTEMAN	*Grilled fish Yemeni-style*

MAIN DISHES

'Meat and fish are fine on the Sabbath, but they are not bad any other day either'

Proverb

The Jewish kitchen has traditionally been poor when it comes to meats
a) because Jews have, for most of the time in their wanderings, been poor and
b) their religious laws forbade the consumption of that versatile meat (beloved of the Chinese and most Europeans) pork as well as certain shell-fish. Therefore those from Europe ate beef, veal, poultry and fish and those from the Orient ate lamb and, to a lesser extent, goat, poultry and fish. However, in Israel all these are available, particularly lamb. All, that is, except pork which goes under the name of 'white beef'. For those who would like to taste the flavour of this forbidden food there is always 'Haze egal ma'oushan' – smoked goose breast, which has all the understood flavours and textures of bacon!

Israel produces some of the finest poultry – all fattened on grain and not fish meal. There is plenty of good fish too – witness the numerous fish restaurants in Tel-Aviv and particularly Haifa.

It is only natural that in a cosmopolitan land such as Israel there is available food from almost every country in the world. One is literally spoilt for choice. Indeed there are more ethnic restaurants in Tel-Aviv and Jerusalem than in such metropolises as London, Paris and New York. What do these establishments serve? The recipes in this chapter are only a fraction of the incredible selection that is now available – if you can afford them. Prices in Israel generally are high and in certain instances, especially in restaurants, extortionate.

The main inspiration of the new Jewish food comes

from the indigenous populace, ie Arabs and Jews from
Arab lands who between them embrace 75 per cent of the
population.

SINEA
Baked minced meat

This is one of the most popular dishes in Israel and is of
Arab origin. Traditionally, 'sinea' – which literally means
tray – is prepared by mixing minced meat and burghul
(cracked wheat) with nuts and spices.

A much simpler version, as in this recipe, is minced
meat with spices and sometimes chopped onion.

      900 g (2 lb) lamb or beef, minced twice
      1 large onion, finely chopped
      1 teaspoon salt
      ½ teaspoon black pepper
      1 teaspoon ground cumin
      1 teaspoon allspice
      25 g (1 oz) butter or margarine
      4 tomatoes, halved
      2 tablespoons tomato purée diluted in 150 ml (¼ pint)
         water
      2 tablespoons finely chopped parsley

1 Place the meat, onion, salt, pepper, cumin and allspice
  in a large bowl and knead thoroughly.
2 Grease a 30 cm (12 in) square baking tray.
3 Spread the meat mixture evenly over the tray so that it
  is about 2.5 cm (1 in) thick.
4 Arrange the halved tomatoes over the meat.
5 Pour the diluted tomato purée over the meat and top
  with a few pats of butter.
6 Cook in a preheated oven; 190°C (375°F) Gas 5, for
  about 1 hour. The meat will shrink away from the sides
  of the tray and will be dark brown in colour.

7 Remove to a large serving dish and cut into squares.
8 Serve with fresh salad and/or roast potatoes.

SINEA CEM TAHINA
Baked minced meat with tahina

The Israelis, who have a penchant for tahina, have created this delicious dish which is, in my opinion, a great improvement on the foregoing recipe.

> 900 g (2 lb) lamb or beef, minced twice
> 1 teaspoon salt
> ½ teaspoon black pepper
> 1 tablespoon Worcester sauce
> 1 tablespoon chives, chopped
> Prepared tahina – see below

> *TAHINA:*
> 110 g (4 oz) dried sesame seeds
> 1 clove garlic
> Juice of 1 lemon
> 150 ml (¼ pint) water
> 2 tablespoons olive oil
> ½ teaspoon salt
> ¼ teaspoon paprika
> Pinch cayenne pepper
> 3–4 tablespoons finely chopped parsley

1 Place all the ingredients for the tahina in a liquidizer and blend thoroughly.
2 Put the meat, salt, pepper, Worcester sauce and chives in a large bowl and knead until thoroughly blended.
3 Butter a 30 cm (12 in) square tray.
4 Spread the meat mixture evenly over the tray so that it is about 2.5 cm (1 in) thick.
5 Pour the prepared tahina over the meat.
6 Bake in a preheated oven, 190°C (375°F) Gas 5, for

about 1 hour or until the tahina is turning a golden brown colour.
7 Place on a serving dish and cut into sections.
8 Serve with salad and/or roast potatoes.

FILET BAKAR DRUCKER
Beef fillet with liver

'What besides beef can you expect from an ox?'

Proverb

Another creation of chef Mordechai Drucker, this is a dish of substance and yet simple and quick to prepare and cook. Serve with grilled tomatoes, sautéed potatoes and a fresh salad.

675 g (1½ lb) beef fillet
Salt
White pepper
4 chicken livers

To serve:
Lettuce leaves

1 Slice the fillet into 4 equal portions.
2 Season on both sides with the salt and pepper.
3 Grill the beef for 6–7 minutes on each side.
4 Meanwhile grill the chicken livers for 3–4 minutes, turning once or twice.
5 Arrange the lettuce leaves on a large plate and place the steaks on top.
6 Top each steak with a chicken liver and serve immediately.

Serves 4

TSLAOT EGAL NUSACH TSAYADIM
Veal cutlets with mushroom sauce

A new dish – by chef Mordechai Drucker – making clever use of veal and mushrooms, which is delicious and looks good. Accompany with vegetables of your choice.

> 8 veal cutlets
> Flour, well seasoned with salt and white pepper
> 350 g (¾ lb) mushrooms, wiped clean and thinly sliced
> oil for frying
> 300 ml (½ pint) white wine

> *To serve:*
> Lettuce leaves

1 Coat the cutlets with the seasoned flour.
2 Heat some oil in a large frying pan or saucepan and fry the cutlets, a few at a time, turning occasionally. If you like your meat medium then fry for about 12 minutes. For a well-done cutlet cook for about 20 minutes.
3 Heat a few tablespoons of oil in a small saucepan and fry the sliced mushrooms for 3–4 minutes.
4 When all the cutlets are cooked, remove them from the pan and keep warm.
5 Add the wine and the sautéed mushrooms to the pan juices and boil for 2 minutes.
6 Arrange the lettuce leaves on a large plate and place the cutlets on top.
7 Pour the sauce into a sauceboat and serve separately.

Serves 4

KEBAB NUSACH ISRAEL
Israeli kebab

Kebabs, of course, are of Middle Eastern origin and this dish falls into that category.

The spicing of kebabs is a matter of taste. While many prefer the flavour of cumin, allspice, coriander or cinnamon, others like the simplicity of just salt, pepper and onion. This recipe I found to be the most popular of all minced lamb kebabs, especially with Israeli Arabs and in the small 'kebab houses' which abound in Jaffa, Tel-Aviv and Jerusalem. The Arabs (the minced kebab is one of their classic dishes) always like to serve the kebab inside a warm pita with a little finely chopped salad, but I prefer it with a rice pilav and salad.

> 675 g (1½ lb) lamb, minced twice
> ¼ teaspoon bicarbonate of soda
> 1 onion, finely chopped
> 1 teaspoon salt
> ½ teaspoon black pepper
> 1 teaspoon allspice
> ½ teaspoon cumin
> 2 tablespoons finely chopped parsley

1 Place all the ingredients in a large bowl and knead until smooth. Dampen your hands with cold water occasionally – this will facilitate the kneading.
2 Form the mixture into a ball, cover and refrigerate overnight.
3 Remove the meat ball from the refrigerator, wet your hands with a little water and form the meat into rolls about 2 cm (¾ in) thick and 7.5–10 cm (3–4 in) long.
4 Place under a hot grill for 10–15 minutes, turning occasionally, until well cooked. (Alternatively, form the rolls around skewers and grill over charcoal. If you

do this, make sure the grill is well oiled to prevent the
meat sticking to it.)
5 Serve either in pitas or with rice and salad.

BASAGH IM BANANA VE TMARIN
Beef stuffed with bananas and dates

There is a classic Aleppan dish called Kafta Mabrouma
which is minced meat rolls with pine kernels. This Israeli
recipe is a far more interesting variation where easily
available local fruits are rolled up in the meat. It is quite
simple to make and it has an exquisite flavour.

The idea of cooking meat with fruit is not new. Persians
and North Africans are past masters, but I believe this
simple approach is new and will spread far beyond the
borders of Israel.

900 g (2 lb) piece of beef – round or flank steak
1 tablespoon prepared mustard
1½ teaspoons salt
½ teaspoon nutmeg
½ teaspoon basil
½ teaspoon black pepper
2 tablespoons ground almonds
2 bananas, peeled and cut into ½ cm (¼ in) slices
2 pickled cucumbers, diced
8 dates, stoned and chopped
8 dried figs, stemmed and chopped
Oil

1 With a wooden mallet pound the meat until about 1 cm
(½ in) thick. Do not over-pound or the meat will tear.
2 Coat the upper surface with the mustard.
3 Mix together the salt, nutmeg, basil, pepper and
ground almonds and sprinkle over the meat.
4 Now cover with the sliced bananas, pickles, dates and
figs.

5 Roll the meat up very carefully.
6 Fasten with string in about three places.
7 Lightly brush the meat all over with oil.
8 Wrap the meat roll in foil and place in a baking pan.
9 Place in the centre of a preheated oven, 190°C (375°F)
   Gas 5, for about 1½ hours or until the meat is tender.
10 Remove from the oven, take off the foil, discard the
   string and serve.

BASAGH KEVIN IM RIMONIM
Lamb with pomegranate

Traditional Middle Eastern cuisines, especially the Iranian and Armenian, have several meat and chicken dishes containing pomegranates or pomegranate juice – for example the Persian 'Fesindjan' (chicken in pomegranate sauce) and the Armenian 'Kharapak khorovadze' (kebab with pomegranate juice) and 'Missov nour' (meat with pomegranates). The recipe given here is a richer version of 'Missov nour' since it includes mushrooms, chives, etc. It tastes delicious and looks spectacular when sprinkled with extra pomegranate seeds.

900 g (2 lb) boned leg of lamb
2 pomegranates
1 large onion, finely chopped
6 mushrooms, washed and thinly sliced
1 tablespoon chives, finely chopped
1 teaspoon allspice
1 teaspoon salt
½ teaspoon black pepper
½ teaspoon sugar
1 tablespoon lemon juice
1 tablespoon tomato purée
600 ml (1 pint) water or stock

1 Cut the pomegranates in half, remove the seeds and reserve them.
2 Cut the meat into 5 cm (2 in) pieces.
3 Put three-quarters of the pomegranate seeds into a bowl together with the onion, mushrooms, allspice, salt, pepper, sugar and lemon juice and mix thoroughly.
4 Line the bottom of a flame-proof casserole dish with half the pomegranate mixture.
5 Arrange the pieces of meat over the top.
6 Cover the meat with the rest of the pomegranate mixture.
7 Dilute the tomato purée in the water or stock and pour it into the casserole.
8 Bring to the boil, cover, lower the heat and simmer for about 1 hour or until the meat is tender.
9 Spoon the mixture into a serving dish and sprinkle the remaining pomegranate seeds over the top.
10 Serve with a rice pilav or roast potatoes.

BASAGH IM KOHLRABI
Kohlrabi stuffed with avocado

Kohlrabi is turnip cabbage, not easy to obtain in Britain although certain specialist shops and a number of oriental shops do sometimes stock it. In the USA Kohlrabi are grown and are widely available.

The green leaves can be cooked in the same way as for spinach beet while the root, which develops above ground, can be peeled and steamed.

12 kohlrabi roots
225 g (½ lb) beef, minced
1 avocado, peeled and the flesh mashed
1 slice white bread, soaked in water and squeezed dry
¼ teaspoon oregano

1 egg
1 teaspoon salt
½ teaspoon black pepper
½ teaspoon cumin
½ teaspoon paprika
1.2 litres (2 pints) tomato juice
1 tablespoon lemon juice
2 bay leaves

For garnish:
2 tablespoons finely chopped parsley
Avocado balls

1 Wash, dry and then trim the kohlrabi roots, removing the leaves and stems.
2 With a sharp knife scoop out the centres of the roots leaving a thin shell, ½–1 cm (¼–½ in) thick, of leaves.
3 Put the meat, mashed avocado, bread, oregano, egg, salt, pepper, cumin and paprika into a large bowl and mix thoroughly.
4 Fill the kohlrabi cases with the mixture.
5 Arrange the stuffed kohlrabi in a large casserole dish.
6 Mix the lemon juice and tomato juice together and pour into the casserole.
7 Add the bay leaves and cover the casserole.
8 Place in a preheated oven, 190°C (375°F) Gas 5, and bake for about 40 minutes, basting occasionally.
9 Place the kohlrabi in a large serving dish and garnish with the parsley and avocado balls.
10 Discard the bay leaves and serve the tomato–lemon sauce separately.

BASAGH EGAL IM MISHMISH
Veal with apricots

This recipe is similar to a classic Arab dish called 'Mish-mishiya' which in turn was most probably derived from the famed Caucasian and North Iranian apricot-based dishes. Veal is an Israeli touch and so is the inclusion of potatoes – altogether a splendid dish with a thick, tasty sauce.

    175g (6 oz) dried apricots, soaked overnight
    4 tablespoons vegetable oil
    1 onion, finely chopped
    2 tablespoons raisins
    2 cloves
    1 tablespoon sugar
    1½ teaspoons salt
    ½ teaspoon cinnamon
    ½ teaspoon white pepper
    350 g (¾ lb) potatoes, peeled and thickly sliced
    350 ml (8 fl oz) water or chicken stock
    450 g (1 lb) boneless veal, sliced into 4 portions

1 Heat the oil in a large flame-proof casserole, add the onion and fry until golden brown.
2 Add the apricots and 5–6 tablespoons of the soaking liquid.
3 Stir in the raisins, cloves, sugar, salt, cinnamon and white pepper.
4 Place the sliced potatoes over the top, add the slices of veal and pour in the water or stock.
5 Bring to the boil, cover the casserole, lower the heat and simmer for about 1 hour or until the meat is tender and the sauce is reduced and thick.
5 Serve immediately with a plain pilav or pita bread and a mixed salad of your choice.

SHASHLIK
Kidney and liver kebab

Shashlik in Russian means marinated, skewered and then grilled lamb – or, as in this recipe, a meat of your choice. It is better known throughout the world as kebab or kobab. Originally Caucasian it is now common throughout the East and West, being popular in Israeli restaurants and using beef fillet, beef liver and lamb kidneys.

I think lamb is by far the best meat for kebab because it is tender, cooks faster and remains succulent, but the choice of meat is of course a very personal one as is the use of vegetables and marinades. The method of cooking is one of the most widespread throughout Israel as well as in the Middle East in general.

I must confess this is a slightly overburdened recipe – although it does look very attractive. I also do not think that kebabs which combine meat and vegetables are always very successful as meat cooks more slowly than tomatoes and green peppers while aubergines will often take longer to be well cooked than meat. As practical considerations must come before appearance I suggest therefore that you skewer the aubergines separately or at least part cook them before putting them with the other ingredients on the skewers.

> 6 lambs' kidneys, halved
> 450 g (1 lb) beef liver, cut into 2.5 cm (1 in) cubes
> 450 g (1 lb) beef fillet, cut into 2.5 cm (1 in) cubes
> Juice of 1 lemon
> 2 tablespoons oil
> 1 teaspoon salt
> ½ teaspoon black pepper
> 1 onion
> 1 large aubergine
> 1 green pepper
> 4 small tomatoes

For garnish:
Lemon wedges
A bowl of fresh salad vegetables

1 Put all the prepared meat into a large bowl.
2 Add the lemon juice, oil, salt and black pepper and mix thoroughly using your hands.
3 Cover and leave in the refrigerator for at least 1 hour.
4 Peel and quarter the onion.
5 Slice 2 quarters of the onion, add to the meat mixture and mix well. This will enhance the flavour of the meat.
6 Separate the layers of the other 2 quarters of onion.
7 Cut the aubergine into 2.5–3.5 cm (1–1½ in) cubes.
8 Remove the core and seeds of the green pepper and quarter it.
9 Skewer alternately a piece of liver, kidney, green pepper, beef fillet, 2–3 pieces of onion, a cube of aubergine etc until the skewers are filled.
10 Insert half a tomato at the very top of each skewer.
11 Place the kebabs under the grill or preferably over charcoal and cook for 15–20 minutes, turning frequently.
12 Serve immediately on a bed of kasha pilav (see recipe, page 201), accompanied by a bowl of fresh salad vegetables.
13 Garnish with the lemon wedges.

DLA'AT MEMULET
Pumpkin stuffed with lamb

'When the sheep are sheared, the lambs tremble'

Proverb

The traditional masters of 'pumpkin cooking' are the people of the Caucasus. Only there is this simple yet very nourishing vegetable used to its fullest potential – pumpkin stews, stuffed pumpkin, pumpkin preserves etc.

This Israeli recipe is undoubtedly of Turkish-Armenian origin as it closely resembles 'kapama'. I remember my grandmother preparing this vegetable when in season, and when it was not available she often substituted cantaloupe or honeydew melon which tasted simply out of this world.

1 small pumpkin
3 tablespoons vegetable oil
225 g (½ lb) minced lamb or beef
1 small onion, finely chopped
110 g (4 oz) cooked rice
2 tablespoons pine kernels
2 tablespoons raisins
1 teaspoon salt
½ teaspoon black pepper
¼ teaspoon curry powder

1 Wash the pumpkin and cut 2.5 cm (1 in) off the top. Reserve the top for later use.
2 Scoop out the seeds and a little of the pulp leaving a shell of skin and pulp about 2 cm (¾ in) thick.
3 Heat the oil in a large saucepan and sauté the meat and onion for 20–30 minutes.
4 Add all the remaining ingredients, mix well and sauté for a further 3 minutes.
5 Spoon this mixture into the pumpkin and cover with the top.
6 Place the pumpkin in a deep baking dish and put into a preheated oven, 180°C (350°F) Gas 4.
7 Bake for 30–40 minutes.
8 Remove the pumpkin from the oven and transfer to a serving dish.
9 To serve cut into portions, spooning additional meat mixture on to each plate.

10 Serve with fresh salad and 'ayran' (watered-down yogourt).

GOULASH TSOANI
Gipsy-style goulash

Gulyás is a Hungarian word which means 'herdsman' or 'cowboy'. It was the traditional dish of the nomadic Magyar races that first settled in that land.

Goulash (unlike the misleading image created by many international recipe books which often suggest it is all paprika and flour) is simply a stew – a one-pan affair traditionally prepared in large cauldrons.

This recipe was created by the chef Arnold Banysh who hails from Rumania and lives in Israel. As the name implies it is gipsy inspired, but it is thoroughly Israeli – another example of the traditional inspiring the new.

2 lambs' hearts
3 lambs' kidneys
1 lamb or beef liver
1 onion, finely chopped
1 teaspoon salt
½ teaspoon black pepper
1 tablespoon parsley, finely chopped
1 tablespoon fresh mint, finely chopped, or 1 teaspoon dried mint
75 g (3 oz) rice, washed thoroughly and drained
Oil for frying

1 Clean the hearts and kidneys thoroughly.
2 Rinse the liver under running water.
3 Arrange the meats in a large saucepan, cover with lightly salted water and bring to the boil.
4 Simmer for 10 minutes.
5 Remove the kidneys and the liver and set aside.

6 Continue simmering the hearts for a further 10 minutes.
7 Remove the hearts and drain.
8 Cut all the meat into 2.5 cm (1 in) cubes.
9 Heat some oil in a large frying pan, add the chopped onion and meat and fry gently, stirring frequently, for 12–15 minutes.
10 Transfer this mixture to another saucepan.
11 Add to the saucepan 3–4 tablespoons water together with the parsley, mint, salt and pepper.
12 Simmer very gently for a further 20–25 minutes, stirring frequently.
13 Stir in the rice, cover and simmer for a further 15–20 minutes or until the rice is tender.
14 Serve with a salad of your choice.

UMTZAT MASADA
Beef fillet in puff pastry

'Better a dish of herbs, where love is than a fattened ox and hatred with it'

Proverb

A tasty and attractive Israeli recipe created by Mordechai Drucker and named in honour of Masada where, in A.D. 70, a group of Jewish zealots held out against the attacking Roman legions and continued to do so for three years. Finally, rather than surrender, they committed mass suicide.

I have cooked this dish several times and find it extremely tasty. I can strongly recommend it, but my personal preference is for an accompaniment of a fresh salad rather than the suggested baked vegetables.

900 g (2 lb) fillet of beef
Oil for frying
225 g (8 oz) mushrooms, washed and chopped

225 g (8 oz) chicken livers, finely chopped
900 g (2 lb) puff pastry
1½ teaspoons salt
½ teaspoon white pepper
1 egg, beaten

For garnish:
Baked marrow, asparagus, glazed carrots or other
  vegetables of your choice

1 Heat some oil in a large pan and gently fry the meat,
  turning frequently, for 20–30 minutes.
2 Remove the meat from the pan and set aside.
3 Fry the chopped mushrooms and liver in the remaining
  oil for about 3 minutes.
4 Season with the salt and pepper and then remove and
  drain on kitchen paper.
5 Roll out the pastry until about ¾ cm (½ in) thick.
6 Place the meat in the middle of the pastry and spread
  the mushrooms and liver on and around it.
7 Close the pastry around the fillet and pinch to seal the
  join. Cut off any extra pastry to use as decoration.
8 Either turn the fillet over so that the join is underneath
  or smooth the pastry over so that the join cannot be
  seen.
9 Place the pastry-enclosed fillet in a large greased
  baking dish.
10 Brush all over with the beaten egg.
11 Decorate with the remaining bits of pastry.
12 Place the meat in a preheated oven, 180°C (350°F) Gas
   4 and bake for about 45 minutes or until golden brown.
13 Set aside to cool for 3–5 minutes and then slice.
   Garnish with the baked vegetables and serve.

HOLISHKES
Stuffed cabbage leaves

Holishkes are stuffed cabbage leaves – a dish popular throughout the Middle East and particularly loved by Turks, Armenians and Arabs. It is also popular in Russia where it is known as 'Galuptzi'.

There are two versions, hot and cold. The basic difference is that the cold version does not have any meat in the filling.

This recipe has a meat filling, is served hot and is of Rumanian origin although it has now become firmly established in the Israeli cuisine.

450 g (1 lb) minced meat
75 g (3 oz) cooked rice
110 g (4 oz) mushrooms, coarsely chopped
1 large onion, grated
2 carrots, grated
1 teaspoon salt
½ teaspoon white pepper
1 egg, beaten
12 large cabbage leaves

For the sauce:
1 tablespoon lemon juice
50 g (2 oz) brown sugar
450 g (1 lb) ripe tomatoes, skinned and sieved or 150g (5 oz) tin tomato purée
300 ml (½ pint) water
2 tablespoons raisins

1 In a large bowl mix together the meat, rice, mushrooms, onion and carrots.
2 Add the salt, pepper and egg and knead until thoroughly blended.

3 Put the cabbage leaves into a large pan of boiling water and cook for 5 minutes.

4 Drain the cabbage leaves and set aside.

5 Place a cabbage leaf on your working surface.

6 Place a tablespoon of the stuffing mixture in a ridge across the leaf near the root end, leaving a clear space of 2.5 cm (1 in) at either end of the leaf.

7 Fold over one end, fold the side edges inwards and then continue to roll up until you have a fat cigar shape, the meat filling being totally enclosed.

8 Stuff and roll up the remaining leaves in similar fashion.

9 Arrange the rolls in a casserole dish, seam sides downwards.

10 Meanwhile, in a small pan mix together the lemon juice, sugar, tomatoes, water and raisins and bring to the boil.

11 Pour the sauce over the rolls. (The sauce should just cover the rolls. If it doesn't then add a little more water.)

12 Weight down the rolls with a heavy plate, cover, place in a preheated oven, 170°C (325°F) Gas 3, and cook for 1½ hours.

13 Uncover the casserole and cook for a further 30 minutes or until the holishkes are nicely browned and the sauce has thickened.

14 Serve immediately, with a fresh salad of your choice.

CHOLENT
Shabbat stew

'He who prepares before the Sabbath can eat on the Sabbath'

Jonathan ben Eleazar

This dish has several names – cholent, shalet, sholent etc and has numerous variations although the basic ingredients remain the same, ie meat, potatoes and fat.

For thousands of years the people of Jewish faith have held the tradition of 'keeping the food hot for the Sabbath', but it was, in fact, in their wanderings throughout Central Europe that the Jewish people mastered one of their classics – the Cholent.

Traditionally the Jews of Poland used potatoes, kasha (see page 201) and, if the family could afford it, a piece of meat. If not – as in most cases – a meat bone was included to give the meal some kind of meaty flavour. As the Jews moved on in their wanderings to new lands, eg Britain, France and the USA, the Cholent too began to change. In Britain beans and barley were added. In the USA today a typical Cholent includes butter beans (lima beans), ginger, paprika, onion, pearl barley etc as well as the traditional potato and meat.

I have included two Cholent recipes, both updated and both highly popular in Israel.

350 g (¾ lb) butter beans (lima beans)
50 g (2 oz) margarine
1.2–1.5kg (2½–3 lb) brisket of beef
1 onion, chopped
1 clove garlic, finely chopped
1 teaspoon salt
½ teaspoon black pepper
¼ teaspoon paprika
¼ teaspoon ginger
¼ teaspoon cinnamon
110 g (¼ lb) pearl barley
10 small potatoes, peeled
2 carrots, peeled and thickly sliced
1 turnip, peeled and cut into 2.5 cm (1 in) pieces
2 bay leaves
1 onion, chopped
1 tablespoon flour
½ tablespoon paprika
Water for boiling

For garnish:
2 tablespoons finely chopped parsley

1 Soak the butter beans in water overnight and then drain.
2 Melt the margarine in a large flame-proof casserole, add the meat, onion and garlic and sauté until brown, turning the meat occasionally.
3 Mix together the salt, pepper, ¼ teaspoon paprika, ginger and cinnamon; sprinkle the mixture over the contents of the casserole and cook, stirring frequently, for 3–4 minutes.
4 Add the beans, pearl barley, the fresh vegetables and bay leaves.
5 Sprinkle with the flour and the ½ teaspoon paprika and stir well.
6 Add sufficient boiling water to cover the ingredients by about 2.5 cm (1 in).
7 Cover the casserole and place in a preheated oven, 180°C (350°F) Gas 4.
8 Cook for 2–3 hours, or until the meat is tender.
9 Remove from the oven, slice the meat and arrange it in the centre of a large serving platter.
10 With a slotted spoon remove the beans, barley and vegetables and arrange them around the meat.
11 Sprinkle with the chopped parsley and serve.
12 Pour the pan juices into a sauceboat and serve as an accompaniment.

Serves 8

CHOLENT IM PEROT
Cholent with fruit

6 dried apricots
20 prunes
900 g (2 lb) brisket of beef

225 g (8 oz) carrots, peeled and cut into ½ cm (¼ in)
    slices
450 g (1 lb) potatoes, peeled and cubed
1 teaspoon salt
½ teaspoon black pepper
Juice of 1 lemon
Grated rind of 1 lemon
50 g (2 oz) honey
Boiling water

For garnish:
Knaidlach dumplings or Mandlen or other small
    pastries of choice (see recipes, pages 97 and 98)
Cooked peas

1 Soak the apricots and prunes in water for 2 hours.
2 Cut the beef into 5 cm (2 in) cubes.
3 Put the pieces of meat, carrots and potatoes into a
   large casserole and season with the salt and pepper.
4 Drain the apricots and prunes, but reserve the
   liquid.
5 Add the fruit to the meat, reserving 5 prunes.
6 Stir in the lemon juice and rind.
7 Mix the honey with a little of the apricot/prune liquid
   and add this mixture to the casserole.
8 Add sufficient boiling water to cover the ingredients by
   about 2.5 cm (1 in).
9 Cover the dish tightly, place in a preheated oven,
   180°C (350°F) Gas 4, and cook for 2–3 hours or until
   the meat is very tender.
10 Meanwhile cook the dumplings and peas.
11 When cooked, transfer the cholent to a large serving
    dish, arrange the cooked peas around the edge and top
    with the dumplings and reserved prunes.

Serves 6–8

One day, the famed Rabbi of Kotzk (Menahem Mendel) read the following passage from the Bible. 'The children of Israel also wept again and said "Who shall give us meat to eat?"' The Rabbi turned round to his congregation, raised his voice and asked 'Why were the children of Israel so angry with Moses? Why did they ask for meat when they had manna? For we are told that each person could taste whatever dish he wanted when he ate manna. So pray tell me why! why! did they insist on meat?'A hush of silence hung all about. Rabbi Mendel looked fiercely at his congregation and continued 'Because the children of Israel were not satisfied with taste alone – they wanted real meat.'

Real meat – that is a subject on which the Yemenites – Muslim, Jewish or the few 'pagans' who live in the highlands – are most knowledgeable. They, of course, make great use of lamb and particularly goat's meat. Not a single part of the animal is wasted – not even the unmentionables! I jest? No; here more for your entertainment and curiosity are some classic Yemenite recipes describing what to do with a lamb's or goat's intestines, udder, shin, tail and penis! I have also included a recipe for grilled locust as an extra inducement for your indulgence. These centuries-old dishes are eaten throughout the Yemen and by those Israeli Jews who try hard to retain their ancient customs. However I did not see a single café or restaurant offering cooked penis – be it ram's, bull's or otherwise – on my stay in the land of milk and honey.

KIRSHEH
Intestines stew

    450 g (1 lb) intestines
    4 tablespoons oil
    1 large onion, chopped

1 clove garlic, chopped
1 teaspoon ground coriander
2 tomatoes, chopped
¼ teaspoon black pepper
½ teaspoon cumin
⅛ teaspoon saffron
2 cardamon pods
1 teaspoon salt

1 Scald the intestines and then clean thoroughly. Boil in water until the meat firms, removing any scum that appears on the surface. Drain and when cool enough to handle cut into cubes.
2 Heat the oil in a large pan, add the onion, garlic and coriander and fry, stirring frequently, until the onion is soft.
3 Add the meat and fry for about 1 hour, stirring frequently.
4 Add the remaining ingredients, mix well, cover the pan and cook over a low heat for about 2 hours, stirring frequently. Add a little water from time to time to prevent sticking.

Serves 4

KAHAL
Spicy udder

450 g (1 lb) udder
1 onion, chopped
1 large tomato, chopped
1 teaspoon salt
1–2 teaspoons hawayij (see recipe, page 94)

1 Wash the meat and then grill until the milk begins to ooze out. Rinse again and then dice the meat.
2 Place the meat in a pan with the remaining ingredients,

add sufficient water to cover and bring to the boil.
Lower the heat and simmer for 3–4 hours or until the
meat is tender. Add a little more water if necessary.

Serves 4

KOR'EE
Shin with hawayij sauce

900 g (2 lb) shin
1 onion, quartered
1 clove garlic, coarsely chopped
1 large tomato, chopped
2–3 teaspoons hawayij (see recipe, page 94)
1 teaspoon salt

1 Rinse the meat and pluck out the hairs. Cut into
portions. Scald in boiling water and then clean again.
2 Place the meat in a large pan with the remaining
ingredients, add enough water to cover and bring to
the boil. Lower the heat and simmer for about 2 hours
or until tender, adding a little more water if necessary.
Traditionally the pan is now placed over a *very* low
flame and left to cook overnight.

Serves 4

GEED
Penis stew

This dish is often served with Schoog (page 196).

450 g (1 lb) penis, ram's or bull's
3 tablespoons oil
1 onion, chopped
2 cloves garlic, chopped
1 teaspoon coriander

1 large tomato, chopped
¼ teaspoon black pepper
1 teaspoon cumin
1 teaspoon salt

1 Scald the penis and clean it. Place in a saucepan, cover with water, bring to the boil and simmer for 10 minutes. Drain and slice the penis.
2 Heat the oil in a large pan, add the onion, garlic and coriander and fry until the onion is golden. Add the penis slices and fry for a few minutes.
3 Stir in the remaining ingredients, add enough water to cover and bring to the boil. Cover the pan, lower the heat and simmer for about 2 hours or until the meat is tender. Add a little water from time to time if necessary, to prevent burning.

Serves 4

LOCUST À LA YEMEN
Dried locusts

1 Heat the oven until very hot and then turn off the heat.
2 Place the locusts on baking trays, place in the hot oven and leave for half a day.
3 Remove from the oven and spread out in the sun to dry for one day.
4 Before eating remove the heads, legs and wings.

KEBAB ME AUFF
Chicken kebab

This is an Israeli kebab adapted from a Greek kebab called 'Stithos Kotas Skharas' which, a Greek friend assures me, is as old as the legend of Venus and the vineyards on the slopes of the Troodos Mountains. Israeli or not, it makes clever use of avocado – a local speciality – as an accompaniment and it does taste excellent.

4 large chicken breasts
2 green peppers, seeded and quartered
2 onions, quartered
2 sticks celery, each cut into 4
4 large mushrooms, washed and trimmed
2 avocados
50 g (2 oz) sugar
1 tablespoon lemon juice
150 ml (¼ pint) red wine
Mint leaves

Marinade:
Juice of 2 lemons
150 ml (¼ pint) cooking oil
150 ml (¼ pint) dry red wine
2 cloves garlic, finely chopped
2 bay leaves
1 teaspoon coriander
1 teaspoon salt
½ teaspoon black pepper

1 Skin and bone the breasts of chicken.
2 Mix together the marinade ingredients, in a large bowl.
3 Add the chicken pieces, turn and leave to marinate overnight in the refrigerator.
4 Remove the chicken breasts from the marinade and thread them on to skewers alternating with pieces of pepper, onion, celery and mushroom.
5 Brush the meat and vegetables with the marinade and grill for 12–15 minutes, turning and basting frequently.
6 While the kebabs are cooking cut the avocados in half lengthways and remove the stones.
7 Mix the sugar, lemon juice and wine together and pour into the halved avocados.

8 Garnish with the mint leaves and serve with the kebabs.

Serves 4

GEFILTE HELZEL
Stuffed neck

This is a unique Jewish speciality illustrating how practical were the Jewish housewives of the Middle Ages when this dish was first evolved.

The neck of a chicken is too small for this dish and so it is best to ask the butcher to let you have a fowl with the neck left intact. The neck is then usually cooked at the same time as the fowl, which can be boiled, roasted or casseroled. However, traditionally, it accompanies a chicken soup.

1 fowl's neck, untorn
50 g (2 oz) plain flour, less 1 tablespoon
1 tablespoon medium matzo meal
3 tablespoons raw chicken fat, finely chopped
2 tablespoons finely chopped onion
1 tablespoon finely chopped parsley
½ teaspoon salt
¼ teaspoon white pepper
Pinch nutmeg

1 Cut the neck from the fowl and remove the skin.
2 Tie or sew up the skin at one end and set aside.
3 Place all the remaining ingredients together in a large bowl. The mixture should be fairly moist, so add a little more chopped fat if necessary.
4 Spoon the stuffing into the neck, but do not pack too tightly as it will swell while cooking.
5 Sew the remaining end up securely.
6 Rinse under cold running water.

7 Pour boiling water over the neck to blanch and smooth the skin.

8 A helzel can be cooked in several ways. It is often roasted in which case it is usually cooked with the fowl. First boil the fowl and the helzel in water for about 1 hour (the stock can be used later for soup) and then place in a roasting tin, brush with oil and cook in the oven for ½–1 hour or until tender and golden.

9 It is very tasty when cooked in a casserole and if done in this way it is not necessary to boil it first.

10 If you wish to cook the helzel in the traditional way then first make a stock for the soup with the fowl or giblets. Remove fowl or giblets, add helzel and simmer in the stock for 30–45 minutes or until tender.

11 When the soup is ready and seasoned, cut the helzel into pieces and serve with the soup.

Serves 2

JEDJAD IMER
Honeyed chicken

'Honey (or sugar) in the mouth won't help bitterness in the heart'

Proverb

A simple and charming dish. The chicken is coated in a honey sauce, giving it a golden sheen and a flavour which is delicate and delightful. This recipe has a strong affinity with several Iranian and Caucasian sweet and sour dishes.

1 × 1.5–1.75 kg (3–4 lb) oven ready chicken, giblets removed and discarded
1 teaspoon salt
½ teaspoon black pepper
Juice of 1 lemon
50 g (2 oz) butter or margarine, melted

4 tablespoons honey
½ teaspoon freshly grated nutmeg

1 Wash and dry the chicken.
2 Rub the chicken with the salt, pepper and lemon juice.
3 In a small bowl mix the melted butter with the honey and the nutmeg until they are thoroughly blended.
4 Using a pastry brush, brush the chicken several times inside and out with this mixture.
5 Put the chicken in a roasting pan and pour the remaining honey sauce over the bird.
6 Place in a preheated oven, 190°C (375°F) Gas 5, and roast until the chicken is tender, basting frequently with the pan juices.
7 Arrange the chicken on a serving dish and pour the pan juices over the top.
8 Carve and serve with an accompaniment of cooked vegetables and roast potatoes.

AUFF MEMULAH NUSACH VIP
Chicken VIP

'It is good to fast – with chicken leg and a bottle of wine'

Proverb

A brilliant creation of chef Mordechai Drucker, this dish requires special attention during its preparation and cooking. It is a simple and original idea – the chicken skin stuffed with a meat mixture.

About 150 ml (¼ pint) vegetable oil
110 g (4 oz) rice, washed thoroughly under cold
    running water and drained
300 ml (½ pint) boiling salted water
1 onion, finely chopped
2 × 900 g (2 lb) chicken
2 tablespoons chopped parsley

110 g (4 oz) chicken liver
2 teaspoons salt
1 teaspoon white pepper
450 ml (¾ pint) boiling chicken stock
25g (1 oz) clear honey
25g (1 oz) French mustard

1 Heat half the oil in a saucepan, add the rice and fry, stirring frequently, until golden brown.
2 Add the 300 ml (½ pint) boiling salted water, stir, transfer to a small casserole dish, place in a preheated oven, 180°C (350°F) Gas 4, and bake for 12–14 minutes.
3 Heat the remaining oil in a small saucepan and sauté the onion until golden brown.
4 To prepare the chicken, skin them with a sharp knife taking care not to break the skin.
5 Separate the thighs and breast.
6 Strip the meat from the bones and mince it with the parsley.
7 Cut the liver into small pieces.
8 Add the chicken flesh and pieces of liver to the sautéed onion and oil in the saucepan.
9 Add the cooked rice and salt and pepper and mix thoroughly.
10 Stuff each chicken skin with the meat-rice mixture.
11 Close the skin and sew up the openings securely with a needle and thread.
12 Place the 'chicken' in a large greased baking dish.
13 Pour the chicken stock into the dish and bake in a preheated oven, 190°C (375°F) Gas 5, for 50–60 minutes.
14 Meanwhile mix the honey and mustard together in a cup.
15 About 10 minutes before the end of the cooking time brush the honey mixture all over the chicken and return it to the oven.

16 When ready to serve, arrange the chicken on a bed of
   lettuce leaves accompanied by vegetables of your
   choice.

AUFF TEMANI
Yemenite chicken

'Roast pigeons don't fly into your mouth'

Proverb

Almost every Yemeni-owned restaurant in Tel-Aviv or
Jerusalem lists this dish on its menu. A tasty dish, it is
simple to prepare and attractive in appearance. The
inclusion of fresh fruit is an Indian influence, as are the
numerous spices.

   4 chicken joints or 1 × 1.5 kg (3 lb) chicken quartered
   4 tablespoons oil
   2 shallots, chopped
   300 ml (½ pint) chicken stock
   1 teaspoon salt
   1 teaspoon allspice
   ½ teaspoon black pepper
   ½ teaspoon cumin
   ¼ teaspoon ginger
   Pinch cloves
   Pinch saffron

   For garnish:
   Chopped parsley
   Slices of pineapple, oranges and bananas

1 Heat the oil in a large flame-proof casserole and fry
   the shallots until soft, stirring frequently.
2 Add the chicken pieces and brown on both sides.

3 Add the chicken stock and all the spices and stir thoroughly.

4 Bring to the boil, cover, lower the heat and simmer for about 1 hour or until the chicken is tender. If necessary add a little more stock.

5 Arrange the chicken pieces on a large serving plate, pour the sauce over the top and sprinkle with the parsley.

6 Arrange the slices of fruit decoratively around the edge of the plate.

Serves 4

GALIL CHAZEH HODU 'MERCHAVIA'
Turkey breasts stuffed with mince meat

The raising of chickens, ducks and especially turkeys is now a major industry in Israel. If you want a whole turkey you have to order it specially – a great number of Sabras (young Israelis) have never seen a whole bird. However, the shops are full of cuts of turkey, chopped turkey pieces for stewing, livers for frying, sliced breast for schnitzel or chopped turkey for making into pâté etc.

This recipe is another of chef Mordechai Drucker's creations.

785 g (1¾ lb) turkey breast
110 g (4 oz) green olives, stoned
1 teaspoon ground ginger
1 egg
½ teaspoon salt
¼ teaspoon white pepper
A few black olives, stoned and chopped
1 chicken-stock cube
50 g (2 oz) margarine, melted
¼ bottle sweet white wine
250 ml (8 fl oz) fresh orange juice

1 Cut 6 slices, about 110g (4 oz) each, from the turkey breast and place on a flat board.
2 Mince the remaining turkey meat with the green olives, ginger, egg, salt and pepper.
3 Arrange a little of this mixture across the centre of each slice of turkey.
4 Roll up each slice and secure firmly, lengthwise, with a toothpick.
5 Coat each turkey roll with a little of the melted margarine.
6 Arrange the rolls in a baking dish.
7 Put the remaining melted margarine in a saucepan and add the stock cube, wine and orange juice.
8 Bring to the boil, make sure that the cube is dissolved and simmer for 5 minutes.
9 Sprinkle the black olives over the turkey rolls and then pour the sauce over the top.
10 Place in a preheated oven, 190°C (375°F) Gas 5, and bake for about 40 minutes.
11 Slice the rolls and arrange the slices on a serving platter.
12 Serve hot with vegetables of your choice.

AUFF MEMULAH IM KASHA
Chicken stuffed with kasha

'A man can live without spices, but not without wheat'

The Talmud

This Russian-inspired dish has been adapted and developed by the Israelis and it appears on many festive tables. I particularly like the local touch of Sabra – incidentally the only liqueur I ever imbibe which I can recommend any time, any place!

1.5–1.75 kg (3–4 lb) oven-ready chicken
6 dried stoned prunes

1 tablespoon sugar
2 tablespoons fat
1 small onion, finely chopped
2 celery sticks, finely chopped
Pinch salt
Pinch white pepper
Pinch paprika
175 g (1 cup) kasha pilav (see recipe, page 201)
3 tablespoons Sabra liqueur

1 Remove and wash the giblets under cold, running water.
2 Put them into a small saucepan with a little water and boil for 5–8 minutes.
3 Drain and allow to cool.
4 Finely chop the giblets and set aside.
5 Boil the prunes in a little water until they are tender.
6 Add the sugar, stir and set aside.
7 Meanwhile in a large saucepan heat the fat and fry the chopped onion until soft.
8 Add the chopped celery, cooked giblets, salt, pepper and paprika and mix well.
9 Now add the kasha pilav and the prunes to the onion mixture.
10 Stir in the Sabra liqueur and mix thoroughly.
11 Rub the inside and outside of the chicken with salt.
12 Spoon the kasha mixture into the chicken and secure the opening. Reserve any surplus pilav and keep warm to serve with the chicken.
13 Place the chicken in a large roasting tin and cook in a preheated oven, 180°C (350°F) Gas 4, for about 1½ hours or until tender. Baste frequently with the juices.
14 Place the chicken on a serving plate and scoop out the stuffing.
15 Garnish the plate with sliced tomatoes and pickled cucumbers.

M.J.C.–G

16 Serve the hot pan juices separately, accompanied by the surplus pilav.

OUGAT AUFF IM TAHINA
Chicken pie

Another new recipe which makes use of tahina and Sabra. A chicken and mushroom filling is encased not in a pastry case, but between layers of tahina sauce.

> *Tahina sauce*
> 6 tablespoons tahina paste
> 300 ml (½ pint) water
> Juice of 1 lemon
> 2 cloves garlic, crushed
> 1 teaspoon salt
> 2 tablespoons finely chopped parsley
>
> *Filling:*
> 110 g (¼ lb) mushrooms, wiped clean
> 3 chicken breasts, boned and minced
> ¼ teaspoon thyme
> ¼ teaspoon rosemary
> 1 teaspoon salt
> 2 tablespoons Sabra liqueur
>
> *For garnish:*
> 8–10 black olives, halved and stoned

1 First prepare the tahina sauce by placing the tahina paste, water and lemon juice in a bowl and mixing until well blended.
2 Add the garlic, salt and parsley and mix thoroughly.
3 Place the mushrooms in a small saucepan with a little water, bring to the boil and then simmer for 5 minutes.
4 Drain the mushrooms and set aside.

5 Put the minced chicken into a bowl together with the thyme, rosemary and salt.
6 Slice the mushrooms thinly and add to the chicken mixture together with the Sabra and about 4 table-spoons of the tahina sauce.
7 Lightly mix the filling ingredients together.
8 Lightly butter a 20 cm (8 in) pie plate.
9 Pour half the remaining tahina sauce into the pie plate.
10 Cover with the chicken mixture and top with the rest of the tahina.
11 Decorate with the olives and bake in a preheated oven 180°C (350°F) Gas 4, for about 45 minutes.
12 Remove from the oven, cut into slices and serve with a salad of your choice.

Serves 4

MUKULI
Chicken with lemon and olives

A traditional Moroccan-Jewish dish. The Israeli cuisine is rich with North African dishes eg Cous-Cous, Tagine and those that are more 'Jewish', ie religious, in conception such as Chicken with Onion or Tfaia and Dafina, served on the Sabbath, or Fish with Carrots served during Chanouka, Festival of Light etc.

There are many North African restaurants in Jerusalem and Tel-Aviv and they, perhaps with the local Palestinian restaurants, serve the finest food to be found in the land.

This recipe – a typical one from the Meghreb – often appears on Israeli hotel and restaurant menus. Its significance is that it has left the family table and become a food of all the people and not just a segment of the nation. It is now (as are most of the dishes in this book) part and parcel of modern Israel.

¼ teaspoon ginger
1 teaspoon cumin
1 teaspoon salt
2 hot chilli peppers
600 ml (1 pint) water
2 tablespoons olive oil
Peel of 1 lemon, white pith removed, cut into thin
　　strips
1 × 1.5–1.75 kg (3–4 lb) chicken, cut into quarters
1 small onion, chopped
4 tablespoons chopped parsley
1 clove garlic, chopped
50 g (2 oz) black olives, soaked in water for 15 minutes
　　to remove salt
60 ml (2 fl oz) lemon juice

For garnish:
Extra black olives

1 Place the ginger, cumin, salt, chilli peppers, water, oil
　and lemon peel in a large pan and bring to the boil.
　Add the chicken pieces and simmer, covered, for 30
　minutes, basting with the liquid occasionally.
2 Place the onion, parsley and garlic in a mortar and
　pound to a paste. Add to the pan, stir well, cover and
　continue to simmer until the chicken is tender.
3 Five minutes before removing from the heat add the
　olives and lemon juice.
4 Serve hot, garnished with the extra olives.

CARPION MEMULA IM GVINAVE PITRINOT
Carp stuffed with cheese and mushrooms

'House guests and fish spoil on the third day'

Proverb

The Jews of Europe took with them to their Holy Land this rather tasteless and bony fish which they spend much time producing. Carp is fried, baked, stuffed or made into gefilte fish (seasoned fish balls). Fish stuffed with cheese and mushrooms is a standard European recipe. The use of carp gives an Israeli touch. Incidentally the best variety of carp – the Mirror or King Carp – is imported into Britain and other European countries from Israel.

1 × 1.75 kg (4 lb) carp, cleaned and washed
150 ml (¼ pint) water
2 tablespoons oil
1 tablespoon finely chopped parsley
2 tablespoons breadcrumbs

For the filling:
50g (2 oz) margarine
1 small onion, finely chopped
6 mushrooms, wiped clean and chopped
2 tomatoes, chopped
50 g (2 oz) grated cheese, Gouda, Stilton or Haloumi
½ teaspoon salt
½ teaspoon black pepper
½ teaspoon marjoram
Pinch cumin

For the sauce:
1 tablespoon flour
2 tablespoons water
300 ml (½ pint) soured cream or yogourt
150 ml (¼ pint) dry white wine
50 g (2 oz) grated cheese, Gouda, Stilton or Haloumi

1 First prepare the filling. Melt the margarine in a saucepan and sauté the onion until soft and translucent.
2 Add the chopped mushrooms, tomatoes, cheese, salt,

pepper, marjoram and cumin, mix thoroughly and cook for about 3 minutes.

3 Remove from the heat and allow to cool for 5 minutes.
4 Rinse the fish under cold running water and pat dry.
5 Spoon the filling into the cavity of the carp.
6 Secure the opening – either with cocktail sticks or small metal skewers.
7 Place the fish in a large, lightly greased baking dish.
8 Add the water, brush the fish with the oil and sprinkle with the parsley and breadcrumbs.
9 Place the fish in a preheated oven, 180°C (350°F) Gas 4, and bake for 30–40 minutes or until the fish turns golden. Baste regularly with the juices in the pan.
10 Meanwhile prepare the sauce by mixing the flour and water in a small bowl.
11 Add the soured cream or yogourt and mix thoroughly.
12 Remove the fish from the oven and pour the sauce over the fish.
13 Sprinkle the cheese over the top.
14 Return the fish to the oven and bake for a further 20 minutes.
15 Serve immediately, accompanied by roast potatoes and fresh salads.

DAG ISRAELI
Israeli cod

'It is the worm that lures the fish, not the fisherman and not the rod'

Proverb

An attractive dish of fried fish served with a pale green avocado sauce. Israel produces great quantities of excellent avocados and the local chefs have created many recipes making use of this exotic fruit. An accompaniment

of fried or jacket potatoes and/or a mixed salad is ideal. I
personally prefer the latter, although I know the Israelis
have a penchant for the former.

75 g (3 oz) flour
2 egg yolks
½ teaspoon salt
¼ teaspoon black pepper
150 ml (¼ pint) beer
½ teaspoon prepared mustard
Oil for frying
8 pieces cod, washed and dried with kitchen paper

For the sauce:
25 g (1 oz) butter
1 small onion, finely chopped
1 clove garlic, crushed
1 large or 2 small ripe avocados
150 ml (¼ pint) water
½ teaspoon salt
¼ teaspoon black pepper
1 tablespoon lemon juice

1 In a bowl blend the flour to a paste with about 6
  tablespoons water.
2 Add the egg yolks, salt and pepper and mix well.
3 Now add the beer and mustard and mix thoroughly for
  a few minutes.
4 Heat some oil in a large frying pan.
5 Dip the fish pieces in the batter, one at a time.
6 Fry the fish, a few pieces at a time, until cooked
  through and golden on both sides.
7 Remove, drain on kitchen paper and keep warm while
  you cook the remainder.
8 Meanwhile prepare the avocado sauce. Melt the butter
  in a small saucepan and sauté the onion and garlic until
  it is transparent.

9 Remove from the heat.

10 Chop the avocado and place in a liquidizer with the onion, garlic, the remaining oil in the pan and the water.

11 Blend until you have a smooth purée and then transfer the mixture back to the saucepan.

12 Season with the salt, pepper and lemon juice and cook over a low heat for 5 minutes, stirring constantly. Add a little more water if the sauce is too thick for your personal taste.

13 Pour the sauce into a sauceboat and serve with the hot fried fish.

Serves 4 or 8, depending on the size of the cod portions.

DAG BE TAHINA
Fish with tahina

The Israelis have taken a great liking to 'tahina'. They have devised several new dishes using this paste of sesame seeds. It is particularly popular with fish, whether fried, baked or stuffed.

I have chosen two typical dishes, both traditional. The first is most certainly Israeli-Jewish while the second is related to the well-known Arab dish 'Samak Bil-Rashi' which is popular in Syria and Jordan as well as among the Palestinians.

Fresh salad is the ideal accompaniment to fish dishes, but a great number of Israelis prefer potatoes in some form or other.

900 g (2 lb) fish – eg bream, whiting, bass etc (either buy ready cut into steaks or buy a whole one and cut it into 8 serving pieces)

1 teaspoon salt

½ teaspoon black pepper

½ teaspoon allspice
2 eggs, beaten
150 ml (¼ pint) oil
2 cloves garlic, coarsely chopped

Tahina
75 g (3 oz) tahina
150 ml (¼ pint) water
Juice of 1 lemon
2 tablespoons chopped parsley

For garnish:
Lemon slices

1 Lightly salt the fish and then refrigerate for 1 hour.
2 Remove the fish from the fridge and rinse under cold running water.
3 Pat dry with kitchen paper and then sprinkle on both sides with the pepper and allspice.
4 Dip each piece of fish in the beaten eggs.
5 Heat the oil in a large pan.
6 Add the fish pieces, a few at a time, and fry until well cooked.
7 When cooked keep the fish warm in the oven.
8 Fry the garlic in the remaining oil.
9 Meanwhile prepare the tahina mixture by combining the tahina with the water, lemon juice and parsley. If it is too thick then add a little more water until you have a thick creamy consistency.
10 With a slotted spoon remove the sautéed garlic from the pan and add it to the tahina mixture.
11 Pour the tahina mixture over the fish and return it to the oven for 10 minutes.
12 Serve immediately garnished with the lemon slices.

Serves 4

DAG BE TAHINA BE EGOZIM
Fish with tahina and nuts

> 4 white fish steaks, eg halibut, cod etc, about 225 g (8
>   oz) each
> ½ teaspoon salt
> Juice of 2 lemons
> About 150 ml (¼ pint) oil
> 2 onions, sliced
> 6 tablespoons coarsely chopped walnuts
> 6 tablespoons tahina paste
> Water
>
> *For garnish:*
> 2 tablespoons finely chopped parsley

1 Wash the fish under cold running water and then pat dry
   with kitchen paper.
2 Sprinkle with the salt and rub in a little of the lemon
   juice.
3 Refrigerate for at least 2 hours.
4 Heat the oil in a large pan and fry the fish until brown.
5 Remove the fish from the pan, drain and place in a
   greased baking dish.
6 Fry the onion in the remaining oil until they are soft.
7 Spread the onion over the fish steaks.
8 Sprinkle the walnuts over the top.
9 In a small bowl mix the tahina with the remaining lemon
   juice until it is creamy. If it is too thick add a little water
   and beat until you have a thick creamy consistency.
10 Pour the tahina mixture over the fish.
11 Place the fish in a preheated oven, 180°C (350°F) Gas 4,
   and bake for about 20 minutes or until the fish is tender.
12 Garnish with the parsley and serve immediately or
   allow to cool.

Serves 4

DAG-YAM-KINNERET
St Peter's Fish

The scientific name of St Peter's fish is *Tilapia Galilaea*. Its large dorsal fin has earned it the popular name of 'comb fish', and because its body is thin, legend has it that its forebears were cloven in two when the Israelites crossed the Red Sea.

This fish is unique to the Sea of Galilee and another legend has it that it is the very fish Peter was gathering when Jesus summoned him away to become a 'fisher of men'. It belongs to the perch family, but tastes more like bream. In Israel it is usually served with French fries, masses and masses of them! I prefer some lemon wedges and a fresh salad. Try both.

    4 small trout, entrails removed, but heads and tails
      intact
    4 sprigs parsley or tarragon
    4 onion slices

Marinade:
6 tablespoons oil
Juice of 1 lemon
1 teaspoon salt
½ teaspoon black pepper
½ teaspoon cumin

1 First prepare the marinade by mixing the ingredients together in a large flat dish.
2 Wash the fish inside and outside, pat dry with kitchen paper and set it in the marinade. Turn in the marinade and then set aside for at least 2 hours to steep.
3 Remove the fish carefully from the marinade and place a sprig of parsley or tarragon and a slice of onion into the cavity of each fish.

4 Grill the fish, brushing regularly with the marinade, for about 15 minutes, turning once.
5 When the skin is crisp and the flesh flaky serve the fish garnished with lemon wedges and accompanied with a fresh salad, or alternatively with French fries.

Serves 4

DAG IM BANAVOT
Fish with bananas

'Don't pat your stomach while the fish is still in the pond'

Proverb

This is a simple dish which is inexpensive, attractive to look at and very tasty.

75 g (3 oz) flour
1 teaspoon salt
½ teaspoon white pepper
110 g (4 oz) unsalted butter
4 halibut steaks or fish of your choice, about 225g (8 oz) each
2 ripe bananas, peeled and halved lengthways
3 tablespoons slivered almonds
3 tablespoons finely chopped parsley
Juice of 1 lemon

For garnish:
3–4 lettuce leaves
Lemon wedges

1 Mix the flour, salt and pepper together on a large shallow plate.
2 Melt about half the butter in a large frying pan.
3 Dip both sides of each fish steak in the flour and place in the pan.

4 Fry gently, turning once, until the fish are golden brown on both sides.

5 Remove the fish to drain on kitchen paper and then reserve in a warm place.

6 Add the remaining butter to the pan and fry the banana halves until they are golden.

7 Arrange a piece of banana on each piece of fish.

8 Fry the almonds in the remaining butter until they are golden.

9 Remove the pan from the heat and stir in the parsley and lemon juice.

10 Arrange the lettuce leaves on a serving plate, place the fish steaks on them and garnish with the lemon wedges.

11 Pour the almond and parsley sauce into a jug and serve with the fish.

Serves 4

DAG METUGAN NO SAKHTEMAN
Grilled fish Yemeni-style

'Grilling fish is no big deal,' said the young Yemeni chef. 'Here we grill fish smothered with dates.'

'Stuffed?'

'No, covered. Oh, sure we have many recipes for fish stuffed with dates, other fruits, rice, nuts etc, but in Yemenite houses we have a very special dish called in Arabic "Samak Mahshi wah Nakhl" – fish in dates. In Hebrew I suppose you can call it "Dag Metugan no Sakhteman".'

He then proceeded to prepare one for me. Here then is chef Sami's (I never discovered his second name) recipe. I hated to upset him then, but it really is just a typical South Arabian dish although fascinating and tasty all the same – sorry, Sami!

175 g (6 oz) dried, stoned dates
6 whole, round, firm-fleshed fish, eg red mullet, each
   about 350g (12 oz), gutted
1 teaspoon salt
2 large onions, finely chopped
2–3 teaspoons hawayij (see recipe, page 94),
   depending on taste

1 Place the dates in a bowl with sufficient water to cover, and set aside for 30 minutes.
2 Rinse the fish thoroughly, pat dry with kitchen paper and then sprinkle with the salt. Set aside for 15 minutes.
3 Meanwhile reduce the dates to a purée with a little of the soaking water either by rubbing through a sieve or by using a liquidizer. Add enough of the water to make a soft paste.
4 Mix the chopped onions and hawayij together with a little water. Stuff each fish with some of this mixture and close the openings with cocktail sticks.
5 Spread the date paste over each side of the fish and place on a greased rack.
6 Cook over charcoal or under a hot grill for 10–12 minutes or until tender, turning once about halfway through the cooking time. Serve with rice or potatoes.

Sauces, Pilavs
and Breads

Sauces, Pilavs and Breads

CHRINE	*Horseradish and beetroot sauce*
TAHINA TARATOR	*Tahina sauce*
SCHOOG	*Yemeni sauce*
ZEMINO SAUCE	*Anchovy and garlic sauce*
YOGOURT IM SHOOM SAUCE	*Yogourt-garlic sauce*
OREZ PILAFF	*Rice pilav*
ROZ SHAMI	*Plain rice pilav*
OREZ PILAFF IM EGOZIM	*Rice with meat, raisins and nuts*
KASHA PILAFF	*Buckwheat pilav*
PITA	*Pita bread*
CHALLAH	*Sabbath bread*
YONTOVDIGE ZIESSE CHALLAH	*Sweet challah*
BAGELS	*Small breads*

SAUCES, PILAVS AND BREADS

'Don't ask for honey cake if you have bread'

Proverb

A good cook is recognized by his or her sauce. A good sauce brings life to cooking and adds that extra flavour to all kinds of dishes. All the well-known sauces used by Western cooks are found in Israel. Some, indeed, are 'overcooked'; eg Bechamel sauce, which appears everywhere and often with dishes that do not (or should not) require its inclusion. However, all said and done there are certain sauces that are Jewish-Israeli in character and these are included here.

CHRINE
Horseradish and beetroot sauce

This is a popular Jewish (chassidim) sauce made of horseradish and beetroot. Serve with lamb and beef kebabs.

    1 small horseradish root
    1 small beetroot
    Salt and pepper to taste
    1 tablespoon white vinegar
    ¼ teaspoon dry mustard
    ½ teaspoon sugar

1 Peel and coarsely grate the horseradish root.
2 Peel and grate the beetroot.
3 Mix the horseradish and beetroot together in a bowl with salt and pepper to taste.
4 Stir in the vinegar, mustard and sugar.
5 Serve as a side dish.

Makes 1 teacupful

TAHINA TARATOR or TAHINIYEH
Tahina sauce

The Israelis, of all the Middle Eastern people, have really succeeded in exploiting tahina – an ingredient that is undoubtedly very new to them. There are several versions of tahina sauce. The recipe below is, in my opinion, the best.

It can be served with fish or kebabs or it can be used in the cooking of chicken, fish etc.

    4 tablespoons tahina paste
    1 clove garlic, crushed
    Juice of 1 lemon
    ½ teaspoon salt
    Pinch paprika
    Pinch cayenne pepper
    250 ml (8 fl oz) water
    2 tablespoons finely chopped parsley

1 Put the tahina, garlic, lemon juice, salt, paprika and cayenne pepper into a bowl and mix well.
2 Gradually add the water, stirring constantly, until the mixture is smooth.
3 Stir in the parsley.

Makes 300 ml (½ pint)

SCHOOG
Yemeni sauce

This is a Yemeni recipe which is very popular in Israel where many Yemeni Jews now live. It is a hot, pungent sauce which can be eaten as an hors d'oeuvre or served with hot vegetable dishes.

    3 cloves garlic
    1 teaspoon cumin

½ teaspoon salt
3 teaspoons ground coriander
6 fresh chillis
2 tomatoes, chopped
Juice of ½ lemon
½ teaspoon sugar
60 ml (2 fl oz) water

1 Blend all the ingredients in a liquidizer.
2 Spoon the mixture into a small saucepan and bring to the boil.
3 Allow to cool and serve in a small bowl or sauceboat as an accompaniment to kebabs, roast meats and/or vegetables.

Makes 150 ml (¼ pint)

ZEMINO SAUCE
Anchovy and garlic sauce

'If you don't eat garlic, you won't smell'

Proverb

This is a strongly flavoured sauce popular with Sephardic Jews – those who originate from Spain and Portugal. It is also popular with the Ladino Jews of Turkey.

This recipe was given to me by a lady who was born in Istanbul, but who now resides with her kin in Beersheba in Israel.

3 tablespoons olive oil
4 cloves garlic, crushed
1 small tin anchovy fillets, very finely chopped or pounded
3 tablespoons breadcrumbs
150 ml (¼ pint) vinegar
2 tablespoons tomato purée

250 ml (8 fl oz) water
¼ teaspoon salt
¼ teaspoon black pepper
¼ teaspoon paprika

1 Heat the oil in a small saucepan and fry the garlic for 2 minutes.
2 Add the chopped anchovies and breadcrumbs and stir well.
3 Gradually add the vinegar, stirring constantly.
4 Dilute the tomato purée in the water and stir into the saucepan.
5 Bring to the boil, stirring constantly.
6 Lower the heat and simmer for about 30 minutes or until the sauce has thickened.
7 Add the seasoning, stir well and serve with any fried fish.

Makes 300 ml (½ pint)

YOGOURT IM SHOOM SAUCE
Yogourt-garlic sauce

This is one of the most popular yogourt-based sauces throughout the Middle East. It is cheap, simple to prepare and will keep in the refrigerator for several days. The sauce is ideal with fried vegetables, eg aubergines, courgettes, spinach etc; with stuffed vegetables and with lamb or beef dishes.

300 ml (½ pint) yogourt
1 clove garlic, crushed
¼ teaspoon salt
½ teaspoon dried mint
1 spring onion, finely chopped

1 Pour the yogourt into a bowl.
2 Mix the garlic and salt together and stir into the yogourt.
3 Mix well to distribute the garlic evenly.
4 Sprinkle the mint and spring onion over the top.
5 Serve chilled.

Makes 300 ml (½ pint)

OREZ PILAFF
Rice pilav

Rice is virtually unknown in Ashkenazim cookery. It only acquires importance in the food of the Oriental Jews and in particular those who originate from the Arab lands and Iran, for rice and the art of cooking it is an integral part of the Middle Eastern cuisine in general, the past masters being the Iranians and Turks.

Today in Israel rice pilav is extremely popular due to the local Arabs. I have therefore included two rice pilav recipes which I found in a great number of restaurants and eating houses. Of course there are several ways of cooking even a plain rice pilav. A general rule when cooking rice is to use 2 cups of liquid for the first cup of rice and 1½ cups of liquid for every additional cup of rice.

ROZ SHAMI
Plain rice pilav

This is called 'Damascus Rice' and is perhaps the simplest and most popular of all plain rice pilavs.

50 g (2 oz) butter
250 g (9 oz/1½ teacups) long grain rice
1 teaspoon salt
600 ml (1 pint/3 cups) boiling stock or water

1 First wash the rice thoroughly under cold running water until the water drains clean.
2 Melt the butter in a saucepan.
3 Add the rice and fry, stirring constantly, for 2–3 minutes.
4 Add the salt and boiling liquid and stir thoroughly.
5 Allow the mixture to boil vigorously for 3 minutes and then cover, lower the heat and simmer for about 20 minutes or until all the liquid has been absorbed. The grains should be separate and tender and there should be small holes in the surface of the rice.
6 Turn off the heat, cover the pan with a clean tea towel, replace the lid and leave to rest for 15 minutes.
7 Carefully fluff up the rice with a long-pronged fork and serve with the dish of your choice.

OREZ PILAFF IM EGOZIM
Rice with meat, raisins and nuts

A rather decorative, delicious pilav ideal for festive occasions. It is very popular with Israelis of Arab origin as well as with Jews from Arab lands.

    450g (1 lb) rice, cooked (see recipe above)
    Oil for frying
    225 g (½ lb) minced meat, lamb or beef
    50 g (2 oz) pine kernels
    50 g (2 oz) chopped almonds
    50 g (2 oz) seedless raisins
    50 g (2 oz) dates, chopped (dried dates will do)
    ½ teaspoon salt
    ¼ teaspoon black pepper
    ½ teaspoon ground cinnamon

1 Prepare the rice as for Roz Shami above.
2 Heat 1 tablespoon of oil in a small saucepan, add the meat and fry for about 10 minutes, stirring frequently.

3 Add 3 tablespoons of water and continue cooking over a low heat for 15–20 minutes or until the meat is soft and crumbly.

4 Meanwhile heat 2–3 tablespoons of oil in a small pan and fry the pine kernels, almonds, raisins and dates for a few minutes until the nuts are golden and the raisins are plump.

5 Stir the nut mixture into the meat and season with the salt, pepper and cinnamon.

6 In a large saucepan heat the rice over a low heat and then add the meat and nut mixture.

7 Mix in well but take care not to break the grains of rice.

8 Serve with meat, fish and poultry dishes.

Serves 6–8

KASHA PILAFF
Buckwheat pilav

'He who holds buckgrain will be cursed by the people,
But blessing will be upon the head of him who sells it'

Proverb

Kasha is the Russian word for cereal and there are scores of kasha dishes, eg kasha with butter, with milk, with salt pork and onions, with eggs, with mushrooms and onions, with pumpkin etc. The recipe given here is a popular one in Israel especially in East European restaurants.

Kasha pilav is a good substitute for rice pilavs and most certainly for potatoes.

225 g (8 oz) whole kasha (buckwheat)
1 egg, beaten
6 tablespoons chicken fat
1 onion, chopped
900 ml (1½ pints) chicken stock

1 teaspoon salt
½ teaspoon white pepper
½ teaspoon paprika
2 tablespoons butter, melted

1 Place the kasha in a large saucepan and brown over a moderate heat, stirring constantly.
2 Add the beaten egg and stir for 2–3 minutes until each grain is nicely separated.
3 Meanwhile in a small saucepan melt the chicken fat, add the onion and sauté until golden brown.
4 Add the onion to the kasha, together with the stock, salt, pepper and paprika.
5 Stir in the butter and bring to the boil.
6 Cover the pan, lower the heat and simmer for 20–25 minutes or until the kasha is tender and the stock absorbed.
7 Stir the kasha several times to allow the moisture to evaporate and to keep the grains separated.
8 Serve as an accompaniment to any meat, or chicken dish of your choice.

PITA
Pita bread

'For bread you can always find a knife'

Proverb

This is undoubtedly the most famous of all Mid-eastern breads. It comes under several names – khubuz Arabi, khubuz Shami, bide, peta or, as it is better known in the West, pita bread.

Pita is perhaps the most popular bread in Israel and can be bought from supermarkets and delicatessens. It is a flat bread, usually round, which when warmed opens up forming a pouch thus making an excellent edible food

container. It is an ideal bread for sandwiches, kebabs or
stuffed with falafel, hot dogs, turkey slices and vegetables.
It is also the ideal bread for eating with hummus, full
medames and other dips.

Interestingly enough this form of bread was well known
in ancient Assyria and most probably the Jews in Exile ate
it those many centuries ago.

 15 g (½ oz) fresh yeast or 8 g (¼ oz) dried yeast
 300 ml (½ pint) tepid water
 Pinch sugar
 450 g (1 lb) plain flour
 ½ teaspoon salt
 Oil

1 Place the yeast and sugar in a small bowl and add 4
  tablespoons of the water.
2 Leave in a warm place until the mixture becomes
  frothy.
3 Sift the flour and salt into a warmed mixing bowl.
4 Make a well in the centre and pour in the frothy yeast
  mixture.
5 Add enough of the tepid water to make a firm, but not
  hard, dough.
6 Flour a working surface and knead the dough for
  about 15 minutes until it is smooth and elastic and no
  longer sticks to your hands.
7 Add a tablespoon of oil and knead a little longer.
8 Wash and dry the mixing bowl and oil it lightly.
9 Roll the dough round and round the bowl until it is
  greased all over.
10 Cover the bowl with a cloth and leave in a warm place
   for about 2 hours or until the dough has about doubled
   in size.
11 Punch the dough down and knead it again for a few
   minutes.
12 Divide the mixture into 8 pieces.

13 Roll each piece around in your hands until round and smooth.
14 Flour the working surface again and flatten each ball of dough with the palm of your hand until it is about 0.6 cm (¼ in) thick and is as even and circular as possible.
15 Dust the loaves with flour and cover with a floured cloth.
16 Leave to rise for about 30 minutes.
17 Preheat the oven to 230°C (450°F) Gas 8, putting in 2 large, oiled baking sheets halfway through the heating period.
18 Slide the rounds of dough on to the hot sheets and dampen the tops to prevent them browning.
19 Bake for 10 minutes; do not open the oven doors during the cooking period.
20 Remove the trays from the oven and place the loaves on a wire rack to cool. They should be soft and white with a pouch inside.

Makes 8 loaves

Pita bread of course is not the only bread available in Israel. There are others. One type in particular, called 'Birgala' or simply 'Kahk', is sold everywhere but is especially popular on the West Bank and in Old Jerusalem. This is a soft, round bread with a large hole in the centre and covered in sesame seeds; it is often sold by street vendors. Another version is about 60cm (2 ft) in diameter and has a much larger hole.

There is, apart from the usual Middle Eastern bread which is a thick round bread found all over the Mediterranean lands, an unusual bread mysteriously named 'Bitha'. It is approximately 2.5 cm (1 in) thick and is either round or long. Although it has a name similar to 'pita' it is, in reality, more like the famed Iranian 'sangak'.

A fascinating bread – really more of a savoury – is one called 'Barazet Naghmin'. It is a very thin, crispy sheet of dough covered in sesame seeds, is sold by street vendors and is related to the famed Damascus biscuits known as 'Barazet Shami'.

The two most famed 'Jewish' breads are, of course, 'Bagels' and 'Challahs'. There are two kinds of challah – a) the everyday version and b) sweet challah, traditionally prepared for special holidays. During the Sabbath meal, which rarely varies, there are always two challah loaves on the table. The custom of two loaves dates back to the Biblical account of the heavenly manna. For on weekdays the children of Israel were ordered to gather only enough for one day, but on the eve of the Sabbath they were commanded to gather two portions of bread, ie for Friday and for Saturday. Whether one is Jewish or not challah is a magnificently tasty, braided bread made from white flour and glazed with egg yolk to give a light brown sheen to the crust.

CHALLAH
Sabbath bread

250 ml (8 fl oz) lukewarm water
1 tablespoon castor sugar
15 g (½ oz) yeast or 2 teaspoons dried yeast
675 g (1½ lb) plain flour
2 teaspoons salt
3 tablespoons oil
1 egg
1 beaten egg yolk
250 ml (8 fl oz) water
2 tablespoons poppy seeds

1 Pour 5–6 tablespoons lukewarm water into a small bowl and add the yeast and sugar.

2 Let the mixture stand for a few minutes so that the yeast dissolves completely.
3 Place the flour in a large bowl, make a well in the centre and add the salt and oil.
4 Break the egg into the well, add the yeast mixture and enough warm water to make a stiff dough.
5 Knead until the dough is smooth and elastic.
6 Cover and leave in a warm place to rise until the dough has about doubled in size.
7 Lightly flour a working surface and knead the dough for a few minutes.
8 Divide the dough into 3 portions – 1 large, 1 medium and 1 small.
9 Taking one portion at a time divide it into 3 equal pieces.
10 Roll each of the pieces into a long 'sausage' and then plait the 3 'sausages'.
11 Repeat the process with the other two lumps of dough.
12 Lay the largest plait on a greased baking sheet.
13 Press the medium plait on to it and the small plait on to that.
14 Brush the surface of the loaf with the beaten egg yolk and sprinkle with the poppy seeds.
15 Bake in the centre of a preheated oven, 180°C (350°F) Gas 4, for about 1 hour or until it sounds hollow when knocked on the bottom.
16 Cool on a wire rack.

Makes a plait about 30 cm (12 in) in length

YONTOVDIGE ZIESSE CHALLAH
Sweet challah

15 g (½ oz) fresh yeast or 2 teaspoons dried yeast
250 ml (8 fl oz) warm water
3½ tablespoons sugar

450 g (1 lb) plain flour
2 teaspoons salt
2 eggs
3 tablespoons oil
50 g (2 oz) raisins

For the glaze:
1 egg yolk

1 Place the yeast in a small bowl with a little of the warm water and 1 teaspoon of the sugar, mix well and set aside until the mixture froths.

2 Sift the flour and salt into a large bowl and make a well in the centre.

3 Pour in the yeast mixture and add the remaining sugar, the eggs and the remaining water. Gradually draw the flour into the liquid until a dough is formed. Add the oil and work in thoroughly. Turn the dough on to a floured surface and knead for 7–10 minutes or until the dough is smooth and elastic. Fold in the raisins and knead until evenly distributed. Shape into a ball.

4 Wash, dry and grease the bowl, add the dough and roll it around the bowl to coat it well with oil. Cover with a tea towel and set aside in a warm place for about 2 hours or until the dough has doubled in size.

5 Punch down the dough, return it to the work surface and knead for a further 2–3 minutes. Return the dough to the bowl, cover and leave to rise again for a further 45 minutes.

6 Punch down the dough again. Place it on the work surface and divide into two portions. Roll each out into a 'sausage' about 60 cm (2 ft) long. Curl each one into a snail shape and place on a greased baking sheet. Cover with a damp cloth and leave to rise for another 30 minutes.

7 Mix the egg yolk with 1 tablespoon water and glaze the
   surface of each loaf.
8 Bake in a preheated oven, 180°C (350°F) Gas 4, for
   about 45 minutes or until golden in colour.

Makes 2 loaves

BAGELS
Small breads

'When you eat a bagel where does the hole go? – into your
pocket!'

Yiddish saying

These are small tasty breads with big holes in the middle,
sold everywhere and munched by everyone. They have
become universally popular, especially in America where
I understand they have become a cult thing – almost the
'American bread'.

This is a typical recipe from Israel as distinct from the
American or, should I say, Ashkenazim version. It uses
sesame seeds instead of poppy seeds and includes ground
caraway. It is a smaller but richer version of the Arab
'birgala'.

   15 g (½ oz) fresh yeast or 2 teaspoons dried yeast
   60 ml (2 fl oz) warm water
   1 teaspoon sugar
   450 g (1 lb) plain flour
   1 teaspoon salt
   1 teaspoon ground caraway
   175 g (6 oz) margarine, melted
   120 ml (4 fl oz) oil

   For the topping:
   1 egg mixed with 1 teaspoon water
   Sesame seeds

1 Place the yeast, water and sugar in a small bowl, mix well and set aside in a warm place for about 10 minutes or until the mixture begins to froth.
2 Sift the flour and salt into a large bowl and stir in the caraway. Make a well in the centre and add the yeast mixture, margarine and oil. Gradually draw in the flour and mix to form a dough. If necessary add just a little more warm water to make a firm dough. Knead for 5–10 minutes or until smooth and elastic.
3 Place the dough in a clean bowl, cover with a tea towel and set aside in a warm place for about 2 hours or until it has doubled in size.
4 Divide the dough into small balls and roll each one into a 'sausage' about 12.5 cm (5 in) long and as thick as a finger. Bring the ends together and pinch to secure.
5 Place on ungreased baking sheets and brush the surfaces with the egg mixture. Sprinkle generously with the sesame seeds.
6 Bake in a preheated oven, 190°C (375°F) Gas 5, for about 20 minutes or until lightly browned. Especially delicious when served straight from the oven.

Makes 30–36

Variation:
Western Jews prepare their bagels by first dropping each one in a pan of simmering water, cooking for 1 minute on each side and then removing to drain. They are then placed on well-greased baking sheets, glazed and baked in a preheated oven, 200°C (400°F) Gas 6, for 40–45 minutes or until light golden.

In Chelm – the famed town of fools – there were no bagels, till one day a delegation was sent to Vilna with the avowed intent of acquiring the secrets of bagel making.

M.J.C.–H

The old baker, Mordecai, explained that there was nothing complicated about it. All they really needed were some holes.

'Now, good friends, put some dough around those holes, simmer them in a pot of boiling water, then straight into the oven and you get bagels.'

'But where do we get the holes from?'

'Ah, I see. Well, you must first buy the bagels from me, then you eat them and keep the holes.'

The members of the delegation bought themselves strings of bagels and set out for home. On the way, as they came to a steep mountain slope, their leader Old Abraham Hesh, said, 'Fellow delegates, we must observe our custom of not carrying anything that can roll down a slope. Let us throw these bagels since they can roll down on their own.'

This they did. Unfortunately for them, there was a pack of hungry dogs who immediately attacked the innocent bagels and devoured them. The Chelmans came down the slope, saw what the dogs were doing and they shouted in unison 'Oy! Oy! For heaven's sake be careful with those holes. Never mind the bagels, preserve the holes. Oy! Oy!'

Drinks

Drinks

AYRAN	*Yogourt drink*
TAPOUZE PUNCH	*Orange punch*
MITZ TOUTIM	*Mulberry syrup*
SAHLAB	*Milk and cinnamon drink*
CAFÉ	*Oriental coffee*
KVASS	*Fermented lemon drink*
VISHNIK	*Cherry drink*

DRINKS

Israel is a land of sobriety – Jew and Arab alike being very
moderate with their drinking. You will see very few, if
any, drunks staggering about the cobbled streets of Jerusalem or Tel Aviv. Both peoples are encouraged not to
drink by religious command. However, this does not
mean that we are confronted with a society so sober as to
be a bore! Israel produces wine, liqueurs and spirits. The
Palestinians have thriving 'arak' and beer distilleries. Jews
are permitted to drink wine on the Sabbath and on special
festive occasions, but generally the populace are sober
(almost) save for a few red-nosed Christians who totter
from one bar to another and, of course, the tourists who,
seated in their hotel lounges, gulp down bottles of 'first
Maccabee beer' while passing their time.

Israelis drink light, soft drinks and they produce many
reasonable juices. All over the land from the smallest
kiosks to the expensive hotels fresh fruit or vegetable
juices are supplied on demand and they are simply
delicious.

One particularly popular drink is 'ayran' which is sold in
ornate brassware containers by street vendors.

AYRAN
Yogourt drink

This is a deliciously refreshing drink particularly on hot
summer days. It was the traditional Middle Eastern cold
drink in the days before the arrival of fizzy juices and cokes!

You can always be sure of a glass of ayran in any Israeli
restaurant, particularly in the small, simple family-run
concerns in Arab Jerusalem.

The proportions given below are for one person. Simply
increase the amounts in proportion to the people catered
for.

2 tablespoons yogourt
300 ml (½ pint) water
¼ teaspoon salt
¼ teaspoon dried mint
Ice cubes

1 Spoon the yogourt into a glass and gradually stir in the water to make a smooth mixture.
2 Add the salt and mint and mix thoroughly.
3 Drop in a few ice cubes and serve.

Serves 1

TAPOUZE PUNCH
Orange punch

'To eat without drinking means suicide'

Sheb 41a

600 ml (1 pint) orange juice
8–9 tablespoons sugar
600 ml (1 pint) strong tea
Juice of 1 lemon
1 orange, peeled and sectioned
Cloves
120 ml (4 fl oz) brandy, preferably peach

1 Heat the orange juice and sugar in a saucepan until the sugar dissolves.
2 Add the tea and lemon juice.
3 Stud 6–8 segments of the orange with cloves and place in the punch mixture.
4 Add the brandy and mix well.
5 Chill for several hours.
6 Serve.

Makes 1.5 litres (2½ pints)

MITZ TOUTIM
Mulberry syrup

Tasty as mulberry,
Sweet as honey is the kiss of my love.
Breasts like pears,
Cheeks of red apples,
Almonds for her brows
Cherries instead of eyes is my love.
Hazel-like limbs,
Hair as palm leaves
Floating, floating, floating
In my dreams – is my love.

Palestinian folk song

I must admit I am rather biased when I say the two most excellent soft drinks in the world are a) sous (made from liquorice wood) and b) mulberry, as I spent a large part of my childhood drinking the juice of this most delightful fruit.

Unfortunately mulberries are not all that easily available in Britain, but in the USA they are abundant. There are several types – the best being Israeli or Syrian – available in good shops. The syrup is concentrated and comes in bottles. To serve, dilute about 1 tablespoon of the syrup in a glass of water and add some ice.

If, by chance, you do find some fresh mulberries I strongly recommend you to make your own syrup, using the method described here.

1 Choose ripe, black mulberries. Wash them and place them in a thin muslin bag.
2 Squeeze the bag gently and leave to drip into a bowl.
3 When all the juice has been extracted measure its volume.
4 Place the juice in a saucepan and add double its volume of sugar.

5 Add 1 tablespoon of lemon juice for every 300 ml (½ pint) of mulberry juice.
6 Bring to the boil, stirring all the time until the sugar has dissolved.
7 Lower the heat and simmer, stirring occasionally, until the syrup thickens. (To check the thickness dip a tablespoon into the syrup. If it coats the back of the spoon then the syrup is thick enough.)
8 Leave the syrup to cool.
9 Pour the syrup into clean bottles, cork securely and store.
10 To serve, simply add 1 tablespoon of the syrup to a glass of water and add some ice.

SAHLAB
Milk and cinnamon drink

A particularly interesting drink, usually sold from kiosks or by street vendors, is sahlab which is made from milk, cornflour, sugar and cinnamon. This is a favourite drink of children who spend their few shekels at the local café or with the street vendors who miraculously appear just when they (the students) are leaving for home. It is a fine refreshing drink which can be drunk warm, but is best chilled.

1.2 litres (2 pints) milk
4 tablespoons cornflour
4 tablespoons sugar
Cinnamon

1 Place the milk and sugar in a pan and heat over a low flame, stirring constantly until the sugar dissolves.
2 In a small bowl mix the cornflour with enough cold water to make a runny paste. Stir in several tablespoons of the warm milk and then pour the contents of

the bowl into the pan, stirring constantly. Continue to
stir until the milk begins to boil.

3 Remove from the heat and leave to cool. Pour into
bowls and sprinkle with the cinnamon. It can also be
garnished with a little dessicated coconut or a few
chopped pistachios.

CAFÉ
Oriental coffee

'What does a pious Jew do before he drinks coffee? – He opens
his mouth.'

American Jewish saying

In Israel today Oriental coffee, ie Arab or Turkish coffee,
is not only drunk by Arabs or Jews, but by a growing
number of Israelis, particularly Sabras. Jews have no
tradition of coffee drinking. Their basic drink was 'chai' –
tea, drunk the Russian way, with no milk, a lick of sugar
and a touch of lemon.

There is only one way of preparing basic Oriental
coffee. This is described below. However there are local
variations:

a) Armenian coffee where, to the basic coffee, 1 cardamon seed and 2 drops of orange flower water are added.

b) Arab coffee which often has added to it a pinch of
saffron and 3–4 cloves.

c) Turkish coffee where a drop or two of rosewater is
often added.

The Greeks, I hasten to add, are satisfied by adding a
few drops of water. The following recipe is for one person
and should be adjusted according to the number of
consumers.

Water
1 teaspoon sugar
1 teaspoon Turkish coffee

1 Measure one cupful of water into a Turkish coffee cup and pour it into a small coffee pot (jaswah). If you are making coffee for a larger number then use a larger jaswah.
2 Stir in the sugar and bring to the boil, stirring until the sugar has dissolved.
3 Add the coffee, stir well and bring to the boil again.
4 As the froth rises remove from the heat and allow the water to descend.
5 Return the jaswah to the heat until the froth reaches the brim and remove once again.
6 Repeat this 3–4 times.
7 Remove from the heat and pour into the appropriate cups.
8 Do not add more sugar and do not stir or you will disturb the thick layer of sediment at the bottom of the cup.

Variation:
The truest coffee of course is the Bedouin coffee. It has a pungent, slightly bitter flavour.

> 1½ coffee cups water
> 1 teaspoon finely ground coffee
> 1 teaspoon sugar
> 1 cardamon pod

1 Place the water in the jaswah. Split the cardamon pod, add to the water and bring to the boil.
2 Remove from the heat, add coffee and sugar, stir and return to the heat until the coffee froths and rises. Remove from the heat until the foam has settled. Return to the heat and then remove again as the foam rises. Continue doing this until the coffee boils without rising. Remove from the heat and pour into a small cup.

Serves 1

Note: Yemenites like to use crushed ginger instead of cardamon while some from North Yemen prefer to flavour their coffee with a little hawayij (see recipe, page 94).

KVASS
Fermented lemon drink

Kvass is a traditional Russian fermented drink usually prepared from rye bread, malt extract, fruit or berry juice with the addition of yeast to aid fermentation, and with mint, lemon or orange rind for flavour. When made, kvass should be stored in a cold place for about two weeks, but not more. If it is left to ferment too long it will not foam when served. It is good for one's digestive system as it kills harmful bacteria and it also makes an excellent appetizer.

There are many kvass recipes. I personally like this lemon–honey kvass which I first tasted in the home of Mr and Mrs Mininsky of Tel-Aviv who gladly gave me their age-old family recipe.

3 litres (5 pints) water
3–4 tablespoons sugar
9 tablespoons honey
Juice and rind of 2 lemons

1 Bring the water to the boil in a large saucepan.
2 Remove from the heat and leave until it has cooled to between 60°–70°C (140°–158°F). You will need a kitchen thermometer.
3 Add the sugar, honey, lemon juice and rind and mix well.
4 Cover the pan and set aside for at least 24 hours.
5 Strain the kvass through cheesecloth or fine muslin.
6 Pour the kvass into bottles, cork and then secure the corks with a slip knot of wire or string.
7 Store in a cool place for about 10 days.

8 At the end of this period the kvass, when served, should be foaming, sparkling and have a pleasant sweet-sour taste.

Makes enough to fill 3 litre (5 pint) bottles

VISHNIK
Cherry drink

This is a Russian drink which is very popular with European Jews. Several Israeli companies manufacture this and similar drinks from the old countries. It is simple to prepare and black cherries or black raspberries can be substituted for the cherries.

450 ml (¾ pint) neutral grain spirits which can be
    bought from wine shops or chemists
1.75 kg (4 lb) sugar
Whole sour cherries

1 Half fill a one-gallon jar with cherries and add the alcohol and sugar.
2 Mix the ingredients thoroughly and cork the jar.
3 Store in a cool place for 1 month.
4 Remove the cork, add more alcohol to fill the jar and then cork loosely.
5 Keep in a cool place for a further 3–4 months.
6 By now the vishnik should be ready.
7 Serve, and Lakaime!

Makes enough to fill 2 litre (3 pint) bottles

Cakes and Sweets

Cakes and Sweets

MISHLACHAT HA NEGEV	*Date rolls stuffed with nuts*
GEREYBES	*Oriental shortbread*
OUGAT GVINA	*Cheesecake*
KICHLACH	*Puffy sweet biscuits*
MOHN KICHLACH	*Poppy seed biscuits*
OZNEI HAMAN	*Deep-fried pastries*
HOMENTASHEN	*Haman's pockets*
MAADAN HASULTAN	*Almond mousse with apricot sauce*
MELON HAROUN EL RASHID	*Melon stuffed with almond mousse and strawberries*
GOUYAVA IM TAHINA	*Guavas with tahina*
KETSIFAT TAPOUZIM	*Orange custard*
TAHINA IM EGOZIM	*Tahina and nut balls*
BASBOUSA	*Semolina cake*
LOKSHEN KUGEL	*Baked noodles with raisins and nuts*
MORATUB TEEN	*Glazed figs*
PUDDING OREZ	*Rice pudding*
MARZIPAN	*Almond paste*
OUGAT GEZER	*Carrot cake*
EINGEMACHTZ	*Radish and honey sweet*
MACAROON SHAKIDIM	*Almond macaroons*

CAKES AND SWEETS

Israel is the Holy Land and Jerusalem is most definitely the city of varied religious festivals, for each of which special sweets and desserts are prepared in quantity and consumed with utter abandon. The Christians, for example, celebrate three different Christmases and Easters; the Muslims have their four-day feast of Aid-al-Fitr, celebrating the end of Ramadan; and then there are the Jewish holidays of Rosh Hashonah, Succoth, Channukah, Purim, Passover and Sharouth – all with special sweets.

In addition to all these religious holidays there are of course the more human and social festivities such as births, weddings and anniversaries. Some groups may treat them more seriously than others, but all try to raise those few hours or days well above the daily norm into something memorable and unforgettable.

We are very fortunate to live in a world that is more just, tolerant and rewarding than ever before. Nothing is perfect and there are many shortcomings, but we (the human race) have, generally, never had it so good. There was a time, not so far back in history, when folk had to wait for such special occasions as weddings, religious festivals etc to treat themselves, with a few dumplings, pancakes, gateaux etc. Today the shops are filled to overflowing with all kinds of sweets, cakes, chocolates, ice creams etc, for we live in the best of all worlds – or so we are constantly reminded by our leaders.

All the famed Middle Eastern sweets are found in Israel, as well as all the well-known Viennese specialities. However, in the last decades new indigenous desserts have been created with success and some I have included here together with the more traditional ones of West and East.

MISHLACHAT HA NEGEV
Date rolls stuffed with nuts

'If you look for cake, you'll lose your bread'

Proverb

This is a creation of chef Roger Debasque. It is typically Oriental and typically Israeli, making use of all local ingredients such as almonds, dates and hazelnuts and dedicated to the 'Negev Expedition'.

It is a good idea to prepare these sweets in large quantities as they will keep for a long time in an airtight tin or glass jar. They are particularly delicious with Turkish coffee or tea.

    4 eggs
    90 ml (3 fl oz) double cream
    600 ml (1 pint) milk
    10 tablespoons sugar
    Green food colouring
    200 g (7 oz) butter
    150 g (5 oz) plain flour
    40 dates, stoned
    150 g (5 oz) shelled hazelnuts
    250 g (9 oz) roasted almonds, chopped
    1 tablespoon vanilla essence
    1 tablespoon almond essence

1 Separate the eggs and reserve the whites for another recipe.
2 Mix the yolks in a small bowl with the cream.
3 Bring the milk to the boil in a saucepan, add the sugar and a drop or two of the colouring until you have a light green hue.
4 In another saucepan melt the butter, add the flour and stir constantly over a low heat until the flour begins to fry.

5 Add the boiled milk gradually, stirring constantly to ensure the mixture is smooth and free from lumps.

6 When the mixture becomes thick, hard and even, stir in the egg yolk mixture.

7 Place in the refrigerator to cool.

8 Stuff each date with 3 whole hazelnuts.

9 When the dough mixture is cool, place on a work surface and knead until pliable.

10 Add the chopped almonds, vanilla and almond essences and knead a little more.

11 Flatten the dough and cut into strips measuring 6 × 1 cm (2½ × ½ in).

12 Fold a strip of dough lengthwise around each date until all the dates have been wrapped in dough.

13 Decorate each sweet with half an almond or walnut.

14 Particularly delicious with Turkish coffee or tea.

Makes 40

GEREYBES
Oriental shortbread

These are delicate plain pastries that literally melt in the mouth and are one of the great classics of the Middle Eastern cuisine, of Syrian origin.

They are simple to make, but do follow the instructions carefully or you may not achieve that 'melting in the mouth' effect.

Traditionally the pastries were heart shaped – hence the Arab name 'lover's sweet'. Now they are usually round or 'S' shaped. They are popular throughout Israel, with the Oriental Jews as well as the Arabs. I also like the Moroccan version which is slightly less sweet but more colourful.

An absolutely delicious pastry with tea or coffee.

450 g (1 lb) unsalted butter
225 g (8 oz) icing sugar, sifted
450 g (1 lb) plain flour, sifted
Blanched almonds

1 Melt the butter in a small saucepan over a low heat.
2 Spoon off any froth and pour the yellow liquid into a bowl leaving any salt residue and water in the saucepan.
3 Place the bowl in the refrigerator and leave until the butter has solidified.
4 Place the butter in a large bowl and beat until it is soft and white. This is a lot easier if you have an electric whisk.
5 Gradually add the icing sugar, beating all the time.
6 Now slowly add the flour and continue mixing until the dough thickens.
7 Collect up the dough with your hand and knead until it is gathered into one smooth ball and is pliable.
8 Leave the dough to rest in the bowl for 10 minutes and preheat the oven to 150°C (300°F) Gas 2.
9 Shape the dough into small walnut-sized balls.
10 Carefully roll out each dough-ball into a 'sausage' and then join the ends to form a circle.
11 Place an almond over the join and gently press.
12 Place the gereybes on a baking sheet, leaving about 2.5 cm (1 in) between each one.
13 Place the baking sheet in the oven and cook until the almonds have turned a light golden, making sure that the gereybes are still white. Under no circumstances must they be overcooked.
14 Remove from the oven and allow to cool.
15 Stored in an airtight tin they will keep a long time. Always handle carefully as they are soft and will easily break.

Makes about 36–40

OUGAT GVINA
Cheesecake

It was perhaps the Greeks who first created 'cheesecake' back on the sunny island of Samos, but with all due respect to the ancient Hellenes it has been the lot of the Jewish housewives to improve, perfect and internationalize this favourite cake of theirs.

Cheesecake had a certain religious symbolism for the Jewish people – the whiteness of milk cheese represented to them the purity of the Mosaic Code. I have selected this particular recipe from scores because it is simple to prepare and because I think it probably comes as near as possible to the original cheesecakes of medieval Jewry.

     4 eggs, separated
     175 g (6 oz) castor sugar
     150 ml (¼ pint) soured cream
     1 tablespoon plain flour
     450 g (1 lb) cottage cheese, sieved
     1 tablespoon semolina
     4 tablespoons sultanas
     1 teaspoon vanilla essence
     Grated rind of 1 lemon
     50 g (2 oz) butter
     6 tablespoons biscuit or sponge crumbs (trifle sponges
        will do very well)
     ½ teaspoon cinnamon

1 In a large bowl, cream together the egg yolks and the sugar until light and smooth.
2 Add the cream, flour, cheese, semolina, sultanas, vanilla essence and lemon rind and beat or whisk for several minutes until well blended and smooth.
3 In a separate bowl whisk the egg whites until stiff.
4 Fold the egg whites into the cheese mixture.
5 Lightly grease a 21–22.5 cm (8½–9 in) cake tin.

6 Melt the butter in a small saucepan and stir in the crumbs and cinnamon.

7 Press this crumb mixture evenly over the base of the tin.

8 Pour the cheese mixture into the tin and smooth over the surface with a wooden spoon.

9 Place in a preheated oven, 180°C (350°F) Gas 4, and bake for 45 minutes. On no account open the oven door during this time.

10 When the cooking time is up turn off the oven, but leave the cake inside to cook for a further 15 minutes.

Serves 8–10

KICHLACH
Puffy sweet biscuits

These little biscuits are ideal for serving with cheese or as party snacks. The same pastry is often used to make strudel or homentashen.

This recipe is a typical one, but there are many variations.

4 eggs
1 teaspoon vanilla essence
2 tablespoons sugar
¼ teaspoon salt
3 tablespoons vegetable oil
350 g (12 oz) flour, half plain and half self raising, sifted
½ teaspoon baking powder

1 Lightly grease 2 large baking trays.

2 Beat the eggs in a mixing bowl together with the vanilla essence.

3 Gradually add half the sugar, then the salt, beating constantly.

4 Add the oil and beat again.
5 Gradually fold in the flour and the baking powder, beating until the mixture forms a pliable dough.
6 Using your hands, knead the dough lightly on a floured surface until it is smooth and elastic.
7 With a floured rolling pin roll out the dough to a large rectangle about 0.6 cm (¼ in) thick.
8 Cut the dough into squares or circles with a pastry cutter.
9 Place the biscuits about 6.5 cm (2½ in) apart on the baking trays.
10 Prick the tops with a fork and sprinkle with the remaining sugar.
11 Place in a preheated oven, 200°C (400°F) Gas 6, and bake for 12–15 minutes or until pale golden in colour.
12 Allow to cool before serving.

Makes about 24

Variation:
This delicious recipe is Mohn kichlach – poppy seed biscuits. They are much sweeter than the above version.

2 eggs, beaten
225 g (8 oz) sugar
175 g (6 oz) margarine
50 g (2 oz) poppy seeds
450 g (1 lb) plain flour
4 teaspoons baking powder
1 teaspoon salt
60 ml (2 fl oz) water

1 Place the eggs, sugar, margarine and poppy seeds in a large bowl and beat or whisk until smooth and creamy.
2 Gradually sift in the flour, baking powder and salt. Add the water and mix until well blended. Gather

together and knead on a work surface until smooth.
Chill.
3 Flour a work surface and roll the dough out until about
3 mm (⅛ in) thick. Use decorative pastry cutters to
make pretty shapes.
4 Place the shapes on greased baking sheets about 2.5
cm (1 in) apart and cook in a preheated oven, 180°C
(350°F) Gas 4, for 10–15 minutes or until lightly
golden.

Quantity depends on size and shape

OZNEI HAMAN
Deep-fried pastries

'Why are there so many Hamans, but only one Purim?' (Haman
tried to exterminate all the Jews of Persia. Purim is the festival
that commemorates Esther's success in foiling Haman.)

These are little pastries fried in oil until crisp. They can be
eaten alone or with ice cream as a dessert.

    2 eggs
    3 tablespoons vegetable oil
    225 g (8 oz) flour, sifted
    Oil for deep frying
    1 tablespoon castor sugar

1 Beat the eggs and vegetable oil together in a mixing
bowl.
2 Gradually add the flour, a little at a time, mixing until
the ingredients form a smooth, soft dough.
3 Lightly flour a working surface and roll out the dough
until it is very thin.
4 Cut the dough into 5 cm (2 in) squares and set them
aside for about 1 hour to dry out.
5 Heat some oil in a frying pan or saucepan until a cube

of dry bread dropped in turns golden in just under a minute.

6 Drop the dough squares into the oil, 2 or 3 at a time, and fry them for about 2 minutes or until they are a light brown.

7 With a slotted spoon remove the pastries from the oil and drain them on kitchen paper.

8 Set aside and keep warm while you fry the rest of the dough squares in the same way.

9 Sprinkle the pastries with castor sugar and serve warm or cold.

Makes about 15

Variation:

An equally famed version is called Haman's pockets or Homentashen. There are those who believe that according to legend Queen Esther could not eat the food served in the Persian Palace (it was not Kosher you see) so she ate seeds (which are permitted by Jewish law). That is why this sweet is stuffed with poppy seeds.

DOUGH:
275 g (10 oz) plain flour
2 teaspoons baking powder
1 teaspoon salt
75 g (3 oz) sugar
4 tablespoons melted butter or margarine
1 egg, beaten
150 ml (¼ pint) milk

Filling 1:
225g (½ lb) poppy seeds
2 eggs, beaten
225 g (½ lb) sugar

Filling 2:
50 g (2 oz) raisins, soaked for 2 hours in water
110 g (4 oz) ground poppy seeds
50 g (2 oz) chopped walnuts or pecans
250 ml (8 fl oz) milk
75 g (3 oz) sugar
2 tablespoons melted butter
1 teaspoon vanilla

Topping:
1 egg yolk mixed with 1 tablespoon water
Icing sugar

1 First choose the filling you wish to use and prepare as follows. *Filling 1* – Rinse the poppy seeds 3–4 times in warm water until the water runs clean. Place the seeds in a saucepan, add enough water to cover by about 5 cm (2 in) and bring to the boil. Lower the heat and simmer for 2 hours. Rinse with cold water and leave to drain until nearly dry. Place in a bowl, add eggs and sugar and mix well. *Filling 2* – Drain the raisins and chop. Place in a saucepan with all the remaining ingredients except the vanilla and cook over a low heat for about 20 minutes, stirring frequently, until the mixture is thick. Set aside to cool and then stir in the vanilla.

2 To prepare the dough sift the flour, baking powder and salt into a large bowl and stir in the sugar. Add the melted butter, egg and milk and mix well.

3 Gather up the dough and knead on a floured work surface until smooth. Flour the work surface and roll out the dough until about 3 mm (⅛ in) thick. Cut into 5 cm (2 in) rounds.

4 Place 1 teaspoon of the chosen filling in the centre of each round and pinch three sides together to make a triangle.

5 Place on greased baking sheets and brush the triangles with the egg yolk-water mixture.

6 Bake in a preheated oven, 180°C (350°F) Gas 4, for about 30 minutes or until golden.

7 Leave to cool and then sprinkle generously with icing sugar.

MAADAN HASULTAN
Almond mousse topped with apricot sauce

A delicious creation by chef Roger Debasque. Extremely attractive to serve.

Custard:
3 eggs, separated
2 tablespoons sugar
300 ml (½ pint) milk

Mousse:
50g (2 oz) toasted almonds, ground
½ teaspoon vanilla essence
½ teaspoon almond essence
Prepared custard, cooled
3 teaspoons gelatine
3 egg whites, remaining from the custard recipe
2 tablespoons sugar
150 ml (¼ pint) cream

Apricot sauce:
225 g (½ lb) fresh ripe apricots, stoned, or 110 g (¼ lb) dried apricots, soaked overnight
Lemon juice
Sugar

Garnish:
6–8 cherries or fresh strawberries

1 To make the custard, place the egg yolks in a small bowl, add the sugar and mix well.

2 Bring the milk to the boil in a small pan. Pour a little of the milk into the egg mixture, stir and then pour back into the rest of the milk in the pan. Stir well and lower the heat.

3 Fill a large saucepan or bowl with cold water and as soon as the milk in the saucepan shows the first sign of boiling, remove it from the heat, dip the pan in the cold water and leave to cool.

4 When the custard is cool proceed to prepare the mousse. Place the ground almonds, vanilla and almond essences and the custard into a large bowl and mix thoroughly.

5 Place the gelatine in a small bowl with a few tablespoons of water, place over a pan of simmering water and stir until dissolved. Stir this into the almond mixture.

6 Whisk the egg whites until stiff and fold in the sugar.

7 Whisk the cream until thick. Fold the egg whites and the cream into the almond mixture with a metal spoon.

8 Either pour the mousse into a large glass dish or into 6–8 individual glasses. (Do not fill more than three-quarters of each glass.) Refrigerate while preparing the apricot sauce.

9 Blend the apricots with a little water to form a purée the consistency of double cream. Add lemon juice and sugar to taste.

10 Pour the sauce over the top of the set mousse. Decorate with the fruit and serve chilled.

Serves 6–8

MELON HAROUN EL RASHID
Melon stuffed with almond mousse and strawberries

The greatest of all Arab khalifs was Haroun el Rashid who was much loved by his people and whose name and fame have become legends in Arabic literature. This recipe, created by chef Roger Debasque, is in honour of this great leader under whose rule all people, especially Jews, were well treated. The dish improves if prepared the day before it is to be served. It is spectacular in appearance and makes an ideal dessert for a dinner party.

> Custard and mousse (see previous recipe)
> 50 g (2 oz) unroasted pistachio nuts
> 3 small round melons, eg cantaloupe or ogen
> 450 g (1 lb) strawberries

1 Prepare the custard and mousse as in the previous recipe, following instructions 1–7 but replacing the ground almonds with whole pistachios (see list of ingredients above).
2 Cut a thin slice, about 0.6 cm (¼ in) thick, off either end of each melon.
3 Scoop a small hole in the top end of each melon and remove and discard the seeds.
4 Rinse each melon with cold water, turn upside down and leave to drain.
5 Pour some of the mousse into each melon.
6 Place some of the strawberries in each fruit (retaining a few for decoration) and then continue to add mousse until each melon is full.
7 Place the melons in the refrigerator until the mousse is set.
8 When ready to serve cut each melon crossways into 2 halves.
9 Place each half into an individual bowl and decorate with strawberries and (if you choose) whipped cream.

GOUYAVA IM TAHINA
Guavas with tahina

Guavas were first introduced into Israel only a decade or
so ago. Today Israel exports a substantial amount of this
exotic fruit and, naturally, the local chefs have experimented with it.

This recipe brings together tahina, figs, coconut and the
Middle Eastern standards – pine kernels and walnuts. The
result is a fascinating and delicious sweet – typically
Israeli.

> 450 g (2 lb) guavas
> 5 tablespoons prepared tahina (see recipe, page 196)
> 150 ml (¼ pint) water
> 110 g (¼ lb) figs, coarsely chopped
> 2 tablespoons shredded coconut
> 2 tablespoons pine kernels
> 2 tablespoons chopped walnuts

> *For garnish:*
> Small bunch grapes
> 2 tangerines, peeled and segmented

1 Cut the guavas in half.
2 With a sharp knife hollow out the insides leaving an
  intact shell about 1 cm (½ in) thick.
3 Discard the pulp.
4 Put the prepared tahina into a small bowl and mix in
  the water.
5 Add the figs, coconut, pine kernels and walnuts and
  mix well.
6 Fill the guavas with this mixture.
7 Chill for a few hours then arrange in a dish, garnish
  with the grapes and tangerine segments and serve.

KETSIFAT TAPOUZIM
Orange custard

A great number of American-created (particularly Cali-
fornian) recipes have entered the Israeli kitchen – this is
one of them. The rich fruit and vegetable agriculture of
California bears a striking relationship to that of Israel
and it is understandable therefore that there are similar-
ities between many of the recipes. This one is simple,
quick and cheap to prepare. It can be made with fruits
other than oranges, eg grapefruit or tangerines. An added
advantage of this sweet is that it will keep in the refrigerator for several days.

    600 ml (1 pint) orange juice
    2 tablespoons lemon juice
    180 ml (6 fl oz) water
    6 tablespoons sugar
    3 tablespoons custard powder mixed with 120 ml (4 fl
        oz) water
    1 tablespoon very finely grated or chopped orange rind
    1 egg, separated

For garnish:
Orange segments

1 Put the orange juice, lemon juice, water and sugar into
  a saucepan and bring slowly to the boil, stirring
  constantly, until the sugar dissolves.
2 Stir in the custard mixture and cook over a low heat for
  about 2 minutes.
3 Remove from the heat and stir in the rind and the egg
  yolk.
4 Whisk the egg white until stiff and fold it into the sweet
  carefully until it is thoroughly blended.
5 Pour into individual dishes or into a serving dish,
  decorate with the orange segments and chill.

TAHINA IM EGOZIM
Tahina and nut balls

This recipe is an adaptation of a very old Armenian sweet
called 'tahinov hatz'. Tahina originated, of course, in
central Anatolia and Cilicia and although it is today a
great favourite with Israelis it has been used in the Middle
East for centuries.

These little cakes are simple and inexpensive to prepare
and will keep for a long time if stored in airtight containers.

Dough:
350 g (12 oz) plain flour
¼ teaspoon salt
110 g (¼ lb) margarine
50 g (2 oz) sugar
Water

Filling:
110 g (¼ lb) crushed walnuts
2 tablespoons finely chopped dates
½ teaspoon cinnamon
1½ tablespoons sugar
3 tablespoons tahina paste

Topping:
1 egg, lightly beaten
Sesame seeds

1 To prepare the dough, first sift the flour and salt into a
   large bowl.
2 Add the margarine and rub it in until the mixture
   resembles fine breadcrumbs.
3 Stir in the sugar.
4 Add a little water at a time and mix, using your hands
   until you have a soft dough.

5 Transfer the dough to a lightly floured surface and knead for a few minutes until it is soft and pliable.

6 Roll it out with a rolling pin until about 6–3 mm (¼–⅛ in) thick.

7 Cut into either 7.5 cm (3 in) squares or circles.

8 Make the filling by mixing together in a bowl the nuts, dates, cinnamon, sugar and tahina paste.

9 Place a large teaspoonful of the filling on each piece of dough and fold as follows.

    a) if the pastry is cut into circles either draw the edges together and roll into balls, or fold the pastry over to form half-moon shapes and seal the edges with a fork.

    b) if the pastry is cut into squares then fold over to form rectangles and seal with a fork.

10 Arrange the cakes on a lightly greased baking tray, brush with the lightly beaten egg and sprinkle with sesame seeds.

11 Place in a preheated oven, 180°C (350°F) Gas 4, and bake for 30–40 minutes or until golden.

12 Leave to cool before serving with tea or coffee.

BASBOUSA
Semolina cake

This is one of the most popular of Middle Eastern sweets. In Greece it is known as 'Sham mali', in Syria as 'Mal Beyrouth', and in Egypt as 'Basbousa'. This semolina-based sweet is simple and cheap to prepare, and is delicious served with coffee or tea.

I spent my early youth in the Middle East and one of my most delightful memories is of the man who used to stand opposite the school with a large tray of 'basbousa' enticing us with its delicate aroma. We had no tuck shops as such in our schools and so the 'basbousa man' was an excellent substitute.

Syrup:
200 ml (⅔ pint) water
225 g (½ lb) sugar
1 tablespoon lemon juice
1 tablespoon rosewater

Cake:
450 g (1 lb) fine semolina
225 g (½ lb) sugar
150 ml (¼ pint) cold water, approximately
150 g (5 oz) unsalted butter, melted
Split almonds

1 First prepare the syrup by putting the water, sugar and
   lemon juice into a pan and bringing to the boil.
2 Lower the heat and simmer until the syrup thickens
   enough to coat the back of a spoon.
3 Stir in the rosewater and set aside to cool.
4 Meanwhile make the cake. First mix the semolina and
   sugar together in a mixing bowl.
5 Pour in the water, a few tablespoons at a time, stirring
   constantly.
6 When the mixture becomes too resistant to stir continue to work in the water with your hand.
7 Add three-quarters of the melted butter and work it
   into the semolina mixture.
8 Grease a 20 × 30 cm (8 × 12 in) baking tin and spoon
   in the semolina mixture.
9 With the back of a spoon spread the mixture evenly in
   the tin.
10 With a sharp knife cut the cake into 5 cm (2 in) squares
   and gently press a split almond into the centre of each
   square.
11 Brush the cake with the remaining butter.
12 Bake in a preheated oven, 180°C (350°F) Gas 4, for
   about 1 hour or until the cake is firm to the touch and
   golden brown.

13 Immediately spoon the syrup evenly over the cake and
   allow to cool before serving.

Makes 24 pieces

LOKSHEN KUGEL
Baked noodles with raisins and nuts

This is perhaps the most famed kugel of them all and one
that is served all over the world on Jewish tables, particularly on the Sabbath. It is a sweet noodle pudding which
can be eaten as a main course in a 'milchig' (dairy dish) or
as a dessert.

Rabbi Pinchas, the Tzaddik of Koritz, was reported to
have quoted on several occasions the following
gourmet-cum-philosophical theorem: Jews eat a great
deal of lokshen on the Sabbath because noodles are
symbolic of the unity of the chosen people; that they are
so entangled they can never be separated.

Personally I think that kugels are a very acquired taste
and that to really appreciate them one has to be brought
up in completely 'Jewish' surroundings. Only then can one
righteously express 'If she can't make a kugel – divorce
her!'

225 g (½ lb) broad noodles
2 eggs, separated
50 g (2 oz) sugar
½ teaspoon cinnamon
¼ teaspoon nutmeg
Pinch salt
3 tablespoons butter or margarine, melted
50 g (2 oz) raisins or chopped apple
25 g (1 oz) chopped walnuts

For the topping:
25 g (1 oz) butter
25 g (1 oz) breadcrumbs

1 Half fill a large saucepan with water and bring to the boil. Add the noodles and cook until tender. Drain.
2 Place the egg yolks in a large bowl with the sugar, cinnamon, nutmeg and salt and beat together. Add the noodles, butter or margarine, raisins or apple and the nuts and mix well.
3 Whisk the egg whites until stiff and fold gently into the noodle mixture.
4 Grease an ovenproof dish and add the noodle mixture. Top with the butter, dotted evenly over the surface and sprinkle with the breadcrumbs.
5 Bake in a preheated oven, 200°C (400°F) Gas 6, for 30–40 minutes or until set and golden.

Serves 4

MORATUB TEEN
Glazed figs

Embrace of the Fig Tree
It stirred its leaves above me and entwined me
in its branches. And at its feet
my small daughter.
I wanted to bend down to her
and the fig tree slapped me with its branches
striking me blind. Light in the room. My daughter
combs her hair sending out sparks.

My God, how can I believe
that she's already twenty.

                                                    Zerubaval Gilead

In this recipe, of Palestinian origin, chopped figs are cooked in a thick syrup. Dates, apricots etc can be prepared in the same way.

Traditionally this sweet is served in small bowls to accompany small cups of Oriental coffee.

450 g (1 lb) dried figs
1 tablespoon lemon juice
175 g (6 oz) sugar
¼ teaspoon ground ginger
¼ teaspoon cinnamon
¼ teaspoon nutmeg
225 g (8 oz) finely chopped walnuts

1 Chop the figs into small pieces and place in a bowl. Add the lemon juice and enough water to cover and leave to soak for 1 hour.
2 Place the figs and liquid in a saucepan and simmer over a low heat until the figs are tender.
3 Add the sugar and spices, mix well and continue to simmer until the syrup is thick and the figs are glazed. Stir in the walnuts and set aside to cool. Store in a covered jar in the refrigerator.

PUDDING OREZ
Rice pudding

A lovely apricot-based rice pudding so typical of Central European cooking at its simple best.

75 g (3 oz) dried apricots, soaked overnight in cold
    water
175 g (6 oz) round-grain rice
600 ml (1 pint) water
75 g (3 oz) sugar
50 g (2 oz) butter or margarine
3 large eggs, separated
½ teaspoon nutmeg
1 teaspoon grated lemon rind
25 g (1 oz) chopped walnuts

1 Drain the apricots and chop into small pieces.
2 Rinse the rice under cold water and place in a sauce-pan with the water. Bring to the boil, lower the heat and simmer for about 12–15 minutes or until only just tender. Do not overcook. Transfer to a sieve and rinse under cold water.
3 Place the butter or margarine in a mixing bowl with the sugar; cream them together until smooth. Beat in the egg yolks one at a time and then stir in the nutmeg, lemon rind, chopped apricots and walnuts. Add the rice and mix in gently.
4 Beat the egg whites until stiff and gently fold into the rice mixture.
5 Pour the mixture into a well-greased ovenproof dish and bake in a preheated oven, 180°C (350°F) Gas 4, for about 45 minutes.
6 Serve hot or cold.

MARZIPAN
Almond paste

Marzipan-type sweets originated, most probably, in Southern Spain and North Africa. The Jews of Spain brought them to the Middle East some two centuries ago. Today marzipan sweets are widely spread throughout the region, being particularly popular in Turkey and Iran.

This paste is traditionally served to a woman who has just given birth, since the almond paste delicacy is considered 'the richest food on earth'.

275 g (10 oz) sugar
250 ml (8 fl oz) water
175 g (6 oz) ground almonds
2 tablespoons lemon juice, strained
1 egg white

For garnish:
Halved blanched almonds

1 Place the sugar and water in a saucepan and bring to the boil, stirring constantly until the sugar has dissolved. Stir in half the lemon juice, lower the heat and simmer until the mixture is syrupy, stirring frequently.

2 Add the ground almonds and continue stirring and scraping around the edges until the mixture forms a ball and is the consistency of a soft dough. Quickly stir in the remaining lemon juice. Remove the pan from the heat and set aside to cool slightly.

3 Meanwhile whisk the egg white until it forms soft peaks. Beat this into the almond mixture and then leave to cool completely, stirring from time to time.

4 Shape the mixture into small balls then roll out and cut into decorative shapes. Place half an almond on top of each sweet.

5 Store in a plastic bag or airtight container.

Makes 30–36 sweets

OUGAT GEZER
Carrot cake

Carrot cake! The idea is not quite as bizarre as it sounds. In fact this recipe is delicious and light.

9 eggs, separated
175 g (6 oz) castor sugar
1 teacup of puréed, cooked carrots
50 g (2 oz) ground almonds
1 tablespoon grated orange rind
1 teaspoon grated lemon rind
2 tablespoons Sabra liqueur
½ teaspoon cinnamon

1 Put the egg yolks into a bowl and beat until smooth.
2 Gradually add the sugar and beat until thick.
3 Add the remaining ingredients (except the egg whites) and stir until well blended.
4 Lightly butter a 20–22.5 cm (8–9 in) round cake tin.
5 Place the egg whites in a bowl and whisk until stiff.
6 Slowly fold the egg whites into the carrot mixture until thoroughly blended.
7 Pour the cake mixture into the tin and smooth over the surface with a wooden spoon.
8 Bake in a preheated oven, 180°C (350°F) Gas 4, about 50 minutes or until golden and firm, but springy to the touch.
9 Remove from the oven and leave to cool in the tin.
10 Remove from the tin and store.

EINGEMACHTZ
Radish and honey sweet

This is another sweet where the main ingredient is a vegetable. There is nothing very unusual in this. Some vegetables do make excellent desserts – witness the brilliant cuisine of the Ottomans, ie the food of the Turks, Armenians, Greeks and Arabs. You will find aubergine, courgette, pumpkin and other vegetable-based sweets.

   The recipe here, though popular with the Ashkenazim Jews of Germany and Poland, was derived a long time ago from similar sweet dishes of Turkey and Iran. In concept it is similar to 'Moratub Teen' (see recipe, page 246).

   675 g (1½ lb) radishes, peeled and chopped
   250 ml (8 fl oz) clear honey
   175 g (6 oz) sugar
   50 g (2 oz) blanched split almonds
   1 tablespoon ground ginger

1 Place the radishes in a large saucepan, add just enough water to cover and bring to the boil. Lower the heat, cover and simmer for 10 minutes. Drain.

2 Return the radishes to the saucepan, add the honey and sugar and stir until the radishes are well coated. Bring to the boil and simmer gently for about 10 minutes or until honey and sugar are well blended. Continue to simmer for about 30 minutes or until the syrup has been absorbed and the mixture is thick and golden.

3 Remove from the heat and stir in the split almonds and ginger. Set aside to cool.

4 Spoon into warm, sterilized jars and seal when completely cold. Store in a cool place.

5 This sweet is usually served in small dishes and eaten with a spoon while drinking tea or coffee.

Makes about 350 g (³⁄₄ lb)

MACAROON SHAKIDIM
Almond macaroons

Also known as 'Mandel Makarones' these are light fluffy sweets that melt in your mouth. A traditional Passover sweet, they are made with matzo meal, orange rind and ground almonds.

75 g (3 oz) ground almonds
4 tablespoons matzo meal
Grated rind of 1 orange
4 egg whites
¼ teaspoon salt
350 g (12 oz) icing sugar

1 Place the almonds, matzo meal and orange rind in a bowl, mix well and set aside.

2 Place the egg whites in a large bowl with the salt and 50 g (2 oz) of the sugar and beat well.
3 Place the remaining sugar in a small saucepan with 2 tablespoons water and bring gently to the boil. Simmer until the syrup is thick and begins to harden – test by dropping a small amount into cold water; if the syrup forms a ball the mixture is ready. While this mixture is still hot gradually add it to the egg whites, beating well after each addition. Continue beating until the mixture is cool.
4 Gently fold in the almond–matzo meal mixture.
5 Place teaspoonfuls of the mixture about 3.5 cm (1½ in) apart on greased baking sheets.
6 Bake in a preheated oven, 160°C (300°F) Gas 2, for 15 minutes. Increase the heat to 180°C (350°F) Gas 4 and cook for a further 15 minutes or until the macaroons are a light golden.

Makes about 40

Before moving on to the next chapter I must mention two other sweets which are well worth knowing about. The first, 'Shaghbiet', are triangular-shaped sweets made with filo pastry and filled with a cream or cheese mixture – absolutely marvellous. They are usually sold by street vendors from large brass trays. Another one of interest is called 'Ash-el-Bulbul' (bird's nest). This is a brilliant concoction of kunafe filo (vermicelli-type pastry) which is shaped like a bird's nest and filled with pistachios. The dough is golden, contrasting with the green of the nuts – marvellous to look at and marvellous to eat.

Festive Specialities

Festive Specialities

SABBATH –
GEFILTE FISH   *Fish balls*
KHAZE KEVES MEMULA   *Stuffed breast of lamb*
LEKACH   *Honey and spice cake*

ROSH HASHONAH –
TZIMMES   *Brisket of beef with*
                                      vegetables
TAYGLACH   *Almond fritters*

SUCCOTH –
KISHUIM MEMULAIM   *Stuffed courgettes*
HAG HA'ASIF TZIMMES   *Pumpkin and fruit stew*

CHANNUKAH –
ISRAEL SOOFGANIYAH   *Fruit doughnuts*
LATKES   *Potato pancakes*

PURIM –
PURIM STOLLEN   *Purim cake*

PASSOVER –
CHAROSETH   *Fruit and nut paste*
MATZO BREI   *Scrambled eggs and*
                                      matzo
MATZO CHICKEN   *Chicken casserole*
STEAK IM YAYN   *Steak in wine*
MATZO KUGEL   *Passover pudding*

RAFREFET TABOUNETZ IM MATZO	*Matzo apple pudding*
GRIMSLICH	*Passover pudding fritters*
VERENIKAS	*Stuffed noodle doughs*
SHAVOUTH –	
KREPLACH	*Patriarch's pastries*
BLINTZES	*Cheese pancakes*
MATZO BLINTZES	*Matzo pancakes*
MAIMOUNA –	
COUS-COUS	*North African beef stew*
FELFEL MEDGOUG	*Roasted red peppers*
ZRODIYA CHALDA	*Carrot salad*
MARMOUNA	*Spicy salad*
SALADE MUGHRABI	*Aubergine salad*

GEFILTE FISH
Fish balls

There are many variations of this classic Ashkenazim dish, which is always present on a Sabbath table. They are usually regional in origin such as 'Litvishe Gefilte Fish' or the famed 'Poilishe Gefilte Fish' – stuffed fish slices Polish-style.

This recipe I have chosen is a simple, standard one which is popular with most European and American Jews.

1.5 kg (3 lb) fish, pike, carp, bream, cod, haddock etc
1½ teaspoons salt
½ teaspoon white pepper
3 carrots, peeled
2 onions, sliced
3 sticks celery with green tops
750 ml (1¼ pints) water
2 thick slices white bread
2 sticks celery, chopped
2 eggs, beaten
1 teaspoon sugar

For garnish:
Lettuce leaves and chopped parsley

1 Skin and bone the fish.
2 Place the heads, skin and bones of the fish in a saucepan.
3 Add half the salt, the pepper, 2 of the carrots, 1 of the sliced onions, the 3 sticks of celery with the green tops and 600 ml (1 pint) of the water.
4 Cook over a low heat for about 1 hour. Add a little more water if necessary.
5 Soak the bread in a little water and squeeze dry.
6 Either blend in a liquidizer or pass twice through a

mincer the boned fish, the remaining carrot and
onion, the chopped celery and the bread.

7 Place the mixture in a large bowl and add the
remaining water, the eggs, the remaining salt and the
sugar.

8 Mix with a wooden spoon or, preferably, your hands.

9 Wet your hands lightly and shape the mixture into
egg-sized balls and set aside.

10 Strain the fish stock through a sieve into another
saucepan. Return the carrots to the stock.

11 Place the fish balls in the stock, and simmer gently for
about 1–1½ hours.

12 Uncover and cook for a further 30 minutes.

13 Remove the saucepan from the heat and leave to
cool.

14 Using a slotted spoon remove the fish balls and place
on a large serving plate.

15 Remove the carrots from the stock, slice them and
arrange the slices decoratively around the fish balls.

16 Pour some of the cooking liquid over the fish balls
and chill thoroughly in refrigerator.

17 Serve garnished with the lettuce leaves and chopped
parsley.

Serves 8

KHAZE KEVES MEMULA
Stuffed breast of lamb

This is a Sephardic dish of Middle Eastern origin. It
appears often on the Sabbath in Jewish homes. It is also
popular with Lebanese, Syrians and Iraqis. Ideal accom-
paniments are a rice pilav and a mixed salad.

1 large breast or 2 small ones (ask your butcher to cut a
    pocket in the breast(s) for the stuffing)
110 g (4 oz) cooked rice
½ teaspoon salt
Pinch black pepper
3 tablespoons coarsely chopped pine kernels or
    walnuts
2 tablespoons chopped parsley
3 tablespoons olive oil
1 tablespoon sifted plain flour
1 teaspoon allspice
450 ml (¾ pint) water

For garnish:
Lettuce, spring onions, radishes etc

1 Trim some of the fat off the breast.
2 Chop some of the trimmed fat into small pieces – use
    about 3 tablespoons – and discard the rest.
3 Put the chopped fat in a bowl with the rice, salt,
    pepper, allspice, nuts and parsley and mix thoroughly.
4 Spoon the stuffing into the pocket of the breast.
5 Close the opening with toothpicks or small metal
    skewers.
6 Heat the olive oil in a large saucepan or frying pan and
    brown the breast all over then remove from the pan.
7 Transfer the breast to an oiled roasting dish.
8 Dust the meat lightly with a little flour.
9 Place in an oven preheated to 180°C (350°F) Gas 4.
10 After 10 minutes add half the water and continue
    roasting for about 40 minutes, after which add the
    remaining water. Baste the meat frequently with the
    pan juices so that the flesh does not become dry.
11 Roast for a further 20–30 minutes or until the meat is
    tender and nicely browned.

12 Serve on a large dish garnished with lettuce, spring onions, radishes etc.

LEKACH
Honey and spice cake

'Rub him with honey and he'll still taste of tar'

Proverb

In Israel this cake is also known as 'Ugat Dvash' and it is one of the musts on the Sabbath. It is a wonderful teatime treat spread with butter.

> 1½ + 1 teaspoons butter
> 275 g (10 oz) + 1 tablespoon flour
> 180 ml (5 fl oz clear honey)
> 50 g (2 oz) soft brown sugar
> 60 ml (2 fl oz) milk
> 3 eggs
> 1 teaspoon bicarbonate soda dissolved in 1 tablespoon milk
> ½ teaspoon ground ginger
> ⅛ teaspoon salt
> ½ teaspoon mixed spice
> ¼ teaspoon ground cloves
> 50 g (2 oz) flaked almonds

1 Preheat the oven to 180°C (350°F) Gas 4.
2 Using the teaspoon of butter, lightly grease a 20 cm (8 in) round cake tin. Sprinkle in the tablespoon of flour, shaking out any excess, and set aside.
3 In a saucepan mix together the honey, sugar and remaining butter and place over a low heat, stirring constantly, until the sugar and butter have dissolved.
4 Remove the pan from the heat and set aside.

5 Place the milk, eggs and soda mixture in a mixing bowl and whisk until frothy.

6 Sift the remaining flour, ginger, salt, mixed spice and cloves into a large mixing bowl.

7 Make a well in the centre and pour in the honey mixture and the milk and egg mixture.

8 Use a metal spoon to mix the liquids together, gradually drawing in the flour.

9 When all the flour has been incorporated and the mixture is smooth, pour the batter into the cake tin.

10 Sprinkle the flaked almonds over the top and place the tin in the centre of the oven.

11 Bake for 1–1¼ hours or until a skewer inserted into the centre of the cake comes out clean.

12 Remove from the oven and leave for 30 minutes in the tin.

13 Turn out on to a wire rack and allow to cool completely before serving.

14 To store, cut into slices and keep in an airtight tin.

Makes one 20 cm (8 inch) cake

TZIMMES
Brisket of beef with vegetables

The Jews were first introduced to sweet and sour cooking while in captivity in Persia. They adapted some of these recipes to suit their very special religious beliefs. Thus was born the honey-based Rosh Hashonah (Beginning of the Year) recipes that cleverly combine sugar and honey with meat and vegetables that appear on this particular day. Indeed, it is traditionally the main item.

This dish is really quite sweet and if you have not tried such a recipe before then cut down a little on the amount of honey you add until your palate becomes used to the flavour.

It is a very attractive dish as the thick honey sauce gives a golden sheen to the meat and vegetables.

> 1 tablespoon fat or margarine
> 900 g (2 lb) brisket of beef
> 3 carrots, peeled and cut into rounds
> 3 sweet potatoes, peeled and thickly sliced
> 3 white potatoes, peeled and thickly sliced
> 1 onion, sliced
> 5–6 tablespoons honey
> 1 teaspoon salt
> ½ teaspoon white pepper
> ¼ teaspoon grated nutmeg
> 1 tablespoon flour

1 Melt the fat in a large saucepan or flame-proof casserole.
2 Add the meat and brown quickly all over.
3 Add the carrots, potatoes, onion, honey, salt, pepper and nutmeg.
4 Add sufficient water to cover and bring to the boil.
5 Lower the heat and simmer for about 3 hours.
6 Transfer the meat to a baking dish.
7 Put the flour in a small bowl, add a few tablespoons of the liquid in the saucepan and mix to a smooth paste.
8 Add this to the liquid and vegetables and mix thoroughly.
9 Pour the liquor and vegetables into the baking dish and place in an oven preheated to 180°C (350°F) Gas 4.
10 Bake for about 45 minutes, basting occasionally, until the meat is nicely browned.

TAYGLACH
Almond fritters

'Eat of the fat and drink the sweet'

Nehemiah

These are traditional Ashkenazim fritters topped with almonds and dipped in a honey and ginger syrup. They will keep a long time if stored in an airtight tin and they are ideal for tea time or as a treat for children.

The Prophet Nehemiah first introduced the Persian custom of 'something sweet' for the month of Tishri, the Jewish New Year, or as it is better known, Rosh Hashonah. It has become a tradition to serve honey and apples all around the festive board. Tayglach were first created with this in mind. They have in time become so popular that now many a Jewish child munches tayglach throughout the year.

110 g (4 oz) flour
1 teaspoon baking powder
¼ teaspoon grated nutmeg
Pinch salt
2 small eggs, beaten

For the syrup:
225 g (½ lb) clear honey
50 g (2 oz) sugar
½ teaspoon ground ginger

For the topping:
25 g (1 oz) chopped almonds

1 Sift together into a mixing bowl the flour, baking powder, nutmeg and salt.
2 Add the beaten eggs and stir to form a stiff dough.

3 Lightly flour a working surface, place the dough on it and knead for 5 minutes until smooth and pliable.
4 Roll out the dough until it is an even 1 cm (½ in) thick and then cut into 2.5 cm (1 in) squares.
5 Make the syrup by mixing the honey, sugar and ginger in a large saucepan and bringing to the boil.
6 Drop a few of the dough squares at a time into the syrup, taking care that it doesn't go off the boil.
7 When all the squares are in and coated with the syrup simmer for about 20 minutes.
8 Remove the tayglachs with a wooden spoon and place on a greased baking sheet.
9 Sprinkle with almonds and pat smooth with the bowl of a wooden spoon dipped in cold water, until they are of an even thickness.
10 When cold cut with a sharp knife into small squares or diamond shapes.

Makes about 20

KISHUIM MEMULAIM
Stuffed courgettes

The feast of Succoth, which is the autumn harvest festival commemorating the years that the Jews had to wander in the Wilderness, is a happy occasion for the Jewish soul. There is a tradition whereby families go on outings to emulate their ancestors. Or else they make their own Tabernacle where they eat their meals.

At this time of the year all kinds of stuffed food are prepared, eg stuffed cabbages, vine leaves, aubergines, pumpkin, kohlrabi, marrows etc. There are several classics among which are 'holishkes' (stuffed cabbage leaves) and 'chatzilim' (stuffed aubergines).

The recipe I have chosen is a relatively new Israeli one which makes use of marrows; it has already acquired the insignia of 'traditional' – and deservedly so.

6 courgettes
450 g (1 lb) minced lamb or beef
1 onion, finely chopped
2 eggs
50 g (2 oz) fresh white breadcrumbs
Oil for frying
1 tablespoon tomato purée
300 ml (½ pint) stock or water
1 teaspoon salt
½ teaspoon black pepper
½ teaspoon sugar

1 Slice the ends off the courgettes and scrape them.
2 Cut each one in half lengthwise.
3 Carefully remove the pulp and place it in the bottom of a saucepan.
4 Place in a large bowl the minced meat, chopped onion and 1 of the eggs. Mix well.
5 Fill the halved courgettes with this mixture.
6 Break the other egg into a shallow basin and beat with a fork.
7 Spread the breadcrumbs out on a plate.
8 One at a time dip the filled, halved courgettes first into the beaten egg and then into the breadcrumbs.
9 Heat some oil in a large frying pan and fry the courgettes until the shells are nicely browned.
10 Dilute the tomato purée in the water and add to the pulp in the saucepan together with the salt, pepper and sugar.
11 Lay the courgettes in the pan, but do not let the sauce cover them.

12 Bring to the boil, cover, lower the heat and simmer for
    about 1 hour or until the meat is tender.
13 Serve immediately with a pilav or potatoes.

HAG HA'ASIF TZIMMES
Pumpkin and fruit stew

This dish is traditionally served at Succoth, the harvest
festival, when the layers symbolize the autumn fruits.
There are many forms of Tzimmes, each one a combination of vegetables or fruit, occasionally with meat added,
but always cooked as slowly as possible to ensure that the
flavours are well blended.

    1 teaspoon vegetable oil
    450 g (1 lb) sweet potatoes, peeled
    450g (1 lb) pumpkin
    1 teaspoon salt
    1 teaspoon black pepper
    ½ teaspoon grated nutmeg
    ¼ teaspoon ground cloves
    6 tablespoons orange marmalade
    3 large cooking apples, peeled, cored and sliced
    2 tablespoons lemon juice
    150 ml (¼ pint) water
    150 ml (¼ pint) white wine
    2 tablespoons grated lemon rind
    1 tablespoon brown sugar
    1 tablespoon butter, cut into small pieces

1 Preheat the oven to 170°C (325°F) Gas 3.
2 Grease a large casserole with the oil and set aside.
3 Place the sweet potatoes in a saucepan, add enough
   water to cover, bring to the boil and then simmer for
   about 20 minutes. Do not allow them to become too
   soft or they will disintegrate.

4 When cooked, drain the sweet potatoes and set aside to cool.

5 Slice the pumpkin, remove the skin and seeds and place the slices in a saucepan.

6 Cover with water, bring to the boil, simmer for 10 minutes and then drain and leave to cool.

7 Place the potatoes and pumpkin on a chopping board and cut into thin slices.

8 Mix together the salt, pepper, nutmeg and cloves.

9 Arrange half the potato slices in the bottom of the casserole.

10 Spread a quarter of the marmalade over the slices and sprinkle with a quarter of the spices.

11 Arrange half the pumpkin slices over the spices and add another quarter of the marmalade and spices.

12 Add the remainder of the potato slices followed by marmalade and spices, then complete the layers with the remaining pumpkin slices topped with the last of the marmalade and spices.

13 Mix the water, wine and lemon juice together and pour over the vegetables.

14 Sprinkle the surface of the casserole's contents with the lemon rind and sugar and dot with the butter.

15 Place in the oven and bake for 1 hour.

16 Serve immediately, on its own as a luncheon dish or as an accompaniment to roast meat.

A MATCHMAKER'S ADVICE

One day a well-known and successful matchmaker (shadchen) was about to take a young groom-to-be to his bride-to-be's house. The young man was not only ignorant of such matters, but was not very bright either.

The matchmaker took him on one side and said 'When

you meet her, open your conversation with the subject of love, then family and only then life and philosophy.'

When our groom-to-be met his future bride he remembered the matchmaker. Seated next to her he whispered 'Do you love Tzimmes?'

'I certainly do,' she answered, puzzled.

Well, thought the young man, that's love settled, now to family. 'Tell me,' he asked 'do you have brothers and sisters?'

'No brother, but two sisters,' she answered.

Good. He had successfully discussed love and family so, looking the young woman in the eyes he spoke. 'Philosophically speaking, tell me, if you did have a brother do you think he would like Tzimmes?'

ISRAEL SOOFGANIYAH
Fruit doughnuts

The Israelis have replaced some of the traditional Channukah (Festival of Lights) specialities (eg potato latkes) with new dishes such as Soofganiyah. This is basically a doughnut, often filled with stoned dates or prunes or with a jam of your choice – reminiscent of European doughnuts.

450 g (1 lb) plain flour
½ teaspoon baking powder
½ teaspoon salt
¼ teaspoon nutmeg
¼ teaspoon cinnamon
110 g (4 oz) sugar
1 egg, beaten
2–3 tablespoons oil
150 ml (¼ pint) milk

15–20 stoned dates, or soaked and stoned prunes, or
    jam of your choice
Oil for frying
Castor sugar

1 Sift the flour twice with the baking powder, salt,
  nutmeg and cinnamon into a large bowl.
2 Stir in the sugar, beaten egg and oil.
3 Commence to knead the mixture, adding sufficient of
  the milk to form a soft dough.
4 Form the dough into walnut-sized balls.
5 With your finger form a depression in each ball and
  tuck in a date or prune or a teaspoon of jam and then
  close the opening and reform the ball.
6 Heat enough oil in a saucepan to deep fry the doughnuts.
7 When hot drop 2 or 3 doughnuts into the oil and cook
  over a moderate heat until well browned all over.
8 Remove with a slotted spoon and drain on kitchen
  paper while the remaining doughnuts are being
  cooked.
9 Sprinkle the doughnuts with castor sugar and serve.

Makes 15–20

LATKES
Potato pancakes

Latkes are pancakes, originally made with cream cheese,
to celebrate Judith's banquet for the Greek general, Ho-
lofernes.

In the 'Pale of Settlement' the Russian Jews substituted
potatoes for cheese. Latkes are traditionally served
straight from the pan and they make a very tasty change

from chips or sautéed potatoes. They are a must on the feast of Channukah – the Feast of Lights.

There are several recipes for this speciality. That given below is a traditional Russian-Jewish one. Some people like their latkes without onion or white pepper – everything is a matter of personal preference.

> 3 large potatoes
> 1 small onion
> 2 small eggs, beaten
> 3 tablespoons self-raising flour
> 1 teaspoon salt
> ½ teaspoon white pepper
> Oil for frying

1 Peel the potatoes and grate finely so that they are reduced almost to a pulp.
2 Place in a sieve to drain for 10 minutes.
3 Meanwhile grate the onion.
4 Squeeze as much liquid as possible from the potato pulp and then place in a mixing bowl.
5 Add the onion to the potatoes.
6 Add the eggs, flour, salt and pepper and mix well until you have a smooth batter.
7 Heat a little oil in a frying pan and when it is hot put in tablespoons of the batter, flattening each with the back of the spoon to make pancakes about 7.5cm (3 in) in diameter.
8 Cook over a moderate heat until brown on one side.
9 Turn and cook on the other side (about 5–7 minutes on each side to allow pancakes to cook through).
10 Remove and drain on kitchen paper.
11 Serve immediately.

PURIM STOLLEN
Purim cake

'Today is Purim – tomorrow it's over –
Fling us a coin, then show us the door!'

Polish Jewish saying

The Purim festival originated about 2,400 years ago in
Persia in the reign of King Ahasuerus in the city of
Shushan. 'Purim' signifies celebration. Traditionally
people must drink to the point where 'they know not
which is Haman and which is Mordecai'.

This is a simple method for preparing the traditional
cake which is filled with a jam and nut mixture of your
choice.

Filling:
Grated rind of 1 lemon
2 tablespoons lemon juice
2 tablespoons sugar
5 tablespoons jam, eg apricot
3 tablespoons chopped hazelnuts or walnuts
50 g (2 oz) poppy seeds

Dough:
1 egg, beaten
5 tablespoons evaporated milk
110 g (4 oz) sugar
110 g (4 oz) finely ground digestive biscuit crumbs
225 g (8 oz) plain flour, sifted
50 g (2 oz) melted butter

1 Put all the filling ingredients in a small bowl and mix
  thoroughly; set aside.
2 Put the egg, milk, sugar, biscuit crumbs, flour and 3
  tablespoons of the melted butter into a large bowl and
  mix thoroughly to form a stiff dough.

3 Flour a working surface, turn out the dough and knead for a few minutes.

4 Flour the working surface again and roll out the dough into a rectangle measuring about 25 × 37.5 cm (10 × 15 in).

5 Brush the surface of the dough lightly with a little of the melted butter.

6 Spread the filling along one of the long sides of the rectangle, 2.5 cm (1 in) from the edge, so that one half of the rectangle is covered.

7 Carefully fold the pastry over the filling and pinch the edges together to completely seal them.

8 Lightly grease a large baking sheet and lift the stollen onto it.

9 Brush the remaining melted butter over the stollen and bake in a preheated oven, 220°C (425°F) Gas 7, for about 20 minutes or until nicely browned.

10 Remove from the oven and cut into slices – diagonally if you like – and serve warm.

Serves 8–10

CHAROSETH
Fruit and nut paste

Under baby's cradle
Stands a golden kid.
The kid went off to trade
With raisins and almonds
Raisins and figs
Baby will sleep hush.

Jewish folk song

There are many variations of this symbolic Jewish sweet which is always included in the Seder – the meal served on

Passover eve. 'Charoseth' recalls the mortar with which the Jews were forced to make bricks when they built the cities of Pithom and Rames for the Egyptians.

Basically the sweets are a mixture of cinnamon, apples or pears and walnuts or pine kernels.

50 g (2 oz) pine kernels
1 hardboiled egg yolk
1 apple, peeled, cored and grated
110 g (4 oz) ground almonds
110 g (4 oz) brown sugar
1 tablespoon grated lemon rind
1 teaspoon ground cinnamon
1 teaspoon ground allspice
3 tablespoons lemon juice
110 g (4 oz) seedless raisins
50 g (2 oz) medium matzo meal

1 Put all the ingredients into a large mixing bowl and mash them to a paste with a fork.
2 Press the mixture evenly into a shallow baking tin.
3 With a sharp knife mark the surface, dividing into an even number of pieces.
4 Place in the refrigerator and chill for at least 30 minutes before cutting it into squares and serving.

Makes about 20–25 sweets

MATZO BREI
Scrambled eggs and matzo

This is a traditional Jewish breakfast dish served during Passover, popular both in Israel and with Western Jewry. There are many variations of this 'French toast', eg fried onions can be added. It is simple and cheap to prepare and delicious to eat. You could even serve it as an after-dinner savoury.

2 matzos broken into 5 cm (2 in) pieces
120 ml (4 fl oz) milk
2 eggs, lightly beaten
½ teaspoon salt
½ teaspoon grated nutmeg
1 tablespoon butter

1 Place the pieces of matzo in a large bowl and pour the milk over them.
2 Leave to soak for about 5 minutes.
3 With a slotted spoon transfer the matzos to another mixing bowl and discard any leftover milk.
4 Pour the eggs on to the matzos.
5 Add the salt and nutmeg and mix well with a wooden spoon.
6 Melt the butter in a frying pan or saucepan and pour in the egg mixture.
7 Cook gently for about 5 minutes, stirring constantly, until the eggs are firm and only slightly moist.
8 Remove from the heat and serve immediately.

Serves 2

MATZO CHICKEN
Chicken casserole

'Are you sure this is kosher for Passover? The price is practically normal.' (Kosher goods tend to be more expensive than normal at this time, mainly due to the tax charged by the Beit-Din.)

A traditional Ashkenazim dish popular in Israel, this is eaten during Passover when no leavened bread may be consumed. It makes an ideal family lunch or informal supper dish, served with a crisp green salad or a pilav of your choice.

8 eggs
1 onion, finely chopped or minced
6 tablespoons chopped fresh dill
4 tablespoons chopped fresh parsley
2 teaspoons salt
1 teaspoon black pepper
½ teaspoon ground mace
450 g (1 lb) cooked chicken meat, cut into strips 1 cm
 wide and 5 cm (2 in long)
225 g (8 oz) mushrooms, wiped clean and chopped
 finely
50 g (2 oz vegetable fat)
5 matzos
450 ml (¾ pint) chicken stock, preferably home-made

1 Preheat the oven to 190°C (375°F) Gas 5.
2 Break the eggs into a large mixing bowl and beat
 lightly.
3 Add the onion, dill, 3 tablespoons of the parsley, the
 salt, pepper and mace.
4 Beat together until the mixture is light and frothy.
5 Add the chicken and mushrooms, mix well and then
 set aside.
6 Melt the fat in a small saucepan over a low heat.
7 Remove the pan from the heat and pour half a
 tablespoon of the fat into a 22.5 cm (9 in) square
 baking tin or dish.
8 Tip and rotate the tin or dish to coat the sides evenly.
9 Reserve the remaining fat.
10 Place the matzos in a large shallow dish, pour the stock
 over them and leave for 1 minute.
11 Remove the matzos from the dish and set aside.
12 Discard any remaining stock.
13 Lay one matzo on the bottom of the tin and cover with
 a quarter of the chicken mixture.

14 Top with another matzo.
15 Repeat this process until all the ingredients are used up, ending with a layer of matzo.
16 Pour the reserved fat over the top matzo, sprinkle with the remaining parsley, and bake for about 30 minutes or until the top is brown.
17 Remove from the oven and serve at once.

STEAK IM YAYN
Steak in wine

Two rabbis sitting in a restaurant drinking wine (needless to say Israeli and kosher). Says one to another '5727 was a good year'.

1 tablespoon oil
1 onion, sliced
450 g (1 lb) shoulder steak, cut into 4 portions
150 ml (¼ pint) dry red wine
150 ml (¼ pint) stock
2 tomatoes, blanched, peeled and sliced
1 clove garlic, crushed
1 teaspoon salt
½ teaspoon white pepper
¼ teaspoon nutmeg

For garnish:
2 tablespoons chopped parsley

1 Heat the oil in a large flame-proof casserole dish, add the onion and sauté until soft and golden.
2 Remove the onion and set aside.
3 Now add the meat to the casserole and brown all over.
4 Remove the steak and set aside with the onions.
5 Stir the remaining ingredients into any oil left in the casserole and bring to the boil.

6 Return the meat to the casserole, turn it in the juices and place the casserole in an oven preheated to 150°C (300°F) Gas 2.
7 Cook for about 2 hours or until the meat is tender and the sauce has thickened.
8 Serve garnished with the parsley and accompanied by rice or potato latkes.

Serves 4

MATZO KUGEL
Passover pudding

'If a woman can't make a kugel – divorce her'

Proverb

A kugel is a pudding usually made of potatoes or noodles and baked in the oven. It originated, like most Ashkenazim dishes, from Central Europe.

50 g (2 oz) + 1 teaspoon butter, melted
6 matzos
350 ml (¾ pint) medium sweet red wine
50 g (2 oz) raisins
50 g (2 oz) almonds, chopped
25 g (1 oz) pine kernels
110 g (4 oz) sugar
½ teaspoon cinnamon
2 teaspoons grated orange rind
4 egg whites
3 tablespoons icing sugar, sifted

1 Preheat the oven to 180°C (350°F) Gas 4.
2 Grease a medium-sized baking dish with the teaspoon of butter and set aside.

3 Crumble the matzos into a small mixing bowl, pour over half the wine and set aside.
4 In another mixing bowl stir together the raisins, almonds, pine kernels, sugar, cinnamon and orange rind.
5 Whisk the egg whites until stiff.
6 Make layers of the matzos (sprinkled with the remaining butter), the raisin and almond mixture and the beaten egg whites.
7 Continue making layers until all the ingredients have been used up, ending with a layer of egg white.
8 Sprinkle the icing sugar over the top and place the dish in the oven.
9 Bake for 25 minutes.
10 Remove the dish from the oven and pour over the remaining wine.
11 Return the dish to the oven and bake for a further 5 minutes.
12 Remove from the oven and serve immediately.

RAFREFET TABOUNETZ IM MATZO
Matzo apple pudding

A simpler variation of the previous recipe this is particularly popular with Hasidic Jews all over the world.

12 matzos
2 cooking apples, peeled, cored and diced
2 tablespoons lard, diced
4 eggs, separated
1 teaspoon cinnamon
½ teaspoon nutmeg
110 g (4 oz) sugar
Pinch salt
50 g (2 oz) blanched almonds, coarsely chopped.

1 Crumble the matzos into a bowl and pour over just enough water to cover. Soak for a few minutes and then squeeze out as much moisture as possible. Transfer to a large mixing bowl. Add the apples and lard and stir well.

2 Beat the egg yolks, add the cinnamon, nutmeg, sugar and salt and mix well. Add to the matzo mixture and stir in the almonds.

3 Whisk the egg whites until stiff and gently fold into the matzo mixture.

4 Pour into a large, greased ovenproof dish.

5 Bake in a preheated oven, 160°C (300°F) Gas 2, for about 1 hour or until the top is golden.

GRIMSLICH
Passover fritters

'Rakusens have just confirmed that the moon rocks gathered by Apollo and Soyuz consist 90 per cent of matzo meal and 10 per cent of ground almonds.'

from the *Treasury of Jewish Quotations*

These fritters are very popular during Passover. There are several variations – as usual – but most have the same basic ingredients, ie matzo, dried fruits, cinnamon and sugar. They are fried in fat – chicken is traditional – sprinkled with sugar and eaten warm. A mid-European doughnut – similar to Arab and Persian fried doughnuts, but lacking the latter's sweetness – they make a fine dessert with a cup of lemon tea.

2 matzos
2 eggs, separated
50 g (2 oz) fine matzo meal
50 g (2 oz) almonds, ground
50 g (2 oz) raisins or sultanas

50 g (2 oz) prunes and/or apricots, chopped
½ teaspoon cinnamon
2 tablespoons fat, melted
50 g (2 oz) sugar

1 Soak the matzos in cold water until soft.
2 Squeeze dry, transfer to a shallow dish and break up with a fork.
3 Beat the egg yolks and add to the matzos together with the matzo meal, almonds, raisins, prunes and/or apricots and the cinnamon.
4 Mix thoroughly.
5 Whisk the egg whites until stiff and fold into the mixture with a metal spoon.
6 Heat the fat in a shallow pan.
7 Drop a few spoonfuls of the batter at a time into the hot fat and fry for a few minutes, turning once, until golden brown on both sides.
8 Remove and drain on kitchen paper while you cook the remaining batter in the same way. Add a little more fat if necessary.
9 Arrange in a serving dish, sprinkle generously with the sugar and serve warm.

VERENIKAS
Stuffed noodle doughs

Once someone asked Mortke Chabad, the wag, 'Tell me, Mortke, you're a smart fellow – why do they call noodles "noodles"?'

Mortke answered without hesitation, 'What a question to ask! They're long like noodles aren't they? They're soft like noodles aren't they? And they taste like noodles don't they? So why shouldn't they be called noodles?'

* * *

Verenikas are filled rounds of noodle dough (similar to kreplach), but they do not quite taste like noodles – they taste a hell of a lot nicer! They are easy to prepare and although recipes tend to vary from family to family the one below is typical and was given to me by an old Polish lady in Tel-Aviv.

2 teacups of mashed potatoes
25 g (1 oz) matzo cake meal
1 teaspoon salt
¼ teaspoon white pepper
3 eggs
1 teacup of cooked minced meat mixed with 2
    tablespoons of pine kernels
50 g (2 oz) medium matzo meal
Oil for frying (chicken fat is ideal)

1 Put the mashed potatoes, cake meal, salt, white pepper and 2 of the eggs into a large mixing bowl and mix thoroughly.
2 Dampen your hands with cold water and form the mixture into small balls about the size of small tomatoes.
3 With a finger make a depression in the centre of each ball.
4 With a teaspoon fill the depressions with the cooked meat and nut mixture.
5 Carefully close each opening by reshaping the potato-meal shells.
6 Roll each ball between your palms and then gently press to slightly flatten.
7 Dip each verenika into the remaining (beaten) egg and then dip each in the matzo meal, making sure that they are well covered.
8 Heat some oil in a large frying pan and fry a few

verenikas at a time, turning only once, to brown on
both sides.
9 Serve immediately with an accompaniment of a fresh
salad for a main meal, or on their own as appetizers.

Serves 4

KREPLACH
Patriarch's pastries

These are triangular pastries said to symbolize the three
Patriarchs: Abraham, Isaac and Jacob. They are usually
eaten on the Eve of the Fast (kol Nidre) and also on the
Feast of Weeks (Shavouth). Although often served with
smetana (soured cream), I prefer them in a nice hot
chicken or meat soup.

Incidentally, the concept of pastries with meat, vegetable or other filling originated in China and the Jews of
Russia most probably took them from the Tartars. The
Turks of course, being of Mongolian extraction, are
famed for their stuffed pastries, 'boregs', which are related to kreplach.

Dough:
225 g (8 oz) plain flour
Pinch salt
2 eggs
3–4 teaspoons water

Filling:
225 g (½ lb) minced beef
1 egg
2 tablespoons grated onion
½ teaspoon salt
Pinch white pepper

1 To make the dough, first sieve the flour and salt into a large bowl.

2 Make a well in the centre, drop in the egg and add the water.

3 Gradually draw the flour into the liquid using a wooden spoon or knife, and then knead for about 5 minutes until you have a smooth dough.

4 Cover the dough with a damp cloth and leave to rest in a warm place for about 20 minutes.

5 Meanwhile make the filling by putting all the ingredients into a bowl and mixing until thoroughly blended.

6 Lightly flour a working surface, divide the dough into 4 portions and roll out one at a time until it is as thin as possible – the thinner the dough the more successful the pastry.

7 When the dough is thin enough – about 1.5 mm (1/16 in) cut it into 5 cm (2 in) squares.

8 Put a teaspoon of the filling on to one corner of each square and fold over to form a triangle.

9 Wet the edges and close firmly either using your fingers or with a fork.

10 Have ready a large sheet of greaseproof paper and lay the kreplach on this as you complete each one.

11 When the kreplach are ready, half fill a large, deep saucepan with water seasoned with salt and bring to the boil.

12 Drop about one third of the kreplach into the boiling water and, after a few minutes, lower the heat, cover the pan and simmer for 30 minutes.

13 Remove the cooked pastries with a slotted spoon and place in a colander.

14 Cook the remaining two thirds of the kreplach in the same way and drain in the colander.

15 The ideal way to serve is to simmer the kreplach in a

meat, chicken or vegetable soup. This will make a very
tasty and filling meal.

BLINTZES
Cheese pancakes

A sweetheart is milk,
A bride is butter
A wife is cheese.

      Ludwig Borne

Blinis are, of course, Russian, but cheese blintzes (as well
as meat or chicken blintzes) are Jewish. They are a must at
any Jewish wedding, festival or other celebration. Blintzes
are very thin pancakes filled with cheese and then fried.

Batter:
110 g (4 oz) plain flour
Pinch salt
2 eggs
1 teaspoon oil
120 ml (4 fl oz) milk
120 ml (4 fl oz) water

Filling:
350 g (¾ lb) curd cheese or sieved cottage cheese
2 tablespoons single cream
1 small teaspoon sugar
Pinch salt

For frying:
Butter and oil

For garnish (optional):
Honey, jam or soured cream

1 Sift the flour and salt into a large bowl, make a well in the centre and add the eggs and the teaspoon of oil.

2 Mix with a wooden spoon until you have a stiff batter.

3 Gradually add the milk and water and continue stirring until a light, smooth batter is formed.

4 Beat or whisk until the surface is covered with bubbles and then set aside for 30 minutes.

5 Now prepare the filling by mixing all the ingredients together thoroughly; set aside until required.

6 To fry the pancakes first pour the batter into a jug. It should be the consistency of single cream and if it is a little thick stir in a few drops of water.

7 Use a 15 cm (6 in) frying or omelette pan which has rounded sides.

8 Heat the pan over a moderate heat for a minute or two then add a teaspoon of oil and swirl it around the base and sides of the pan.

9 Make a small pad out of a piece of kitchen paper and wipe away any excess oil.

10 Now use the pad to smear butter very thinly over the entire surface of the pan.

11 Pour a thick layer of the batter into the pan and swirl it around so that it covers the sides as well as the base.

12 The heat will set a thin layer and the excess can then be poured back into the jug.

13 When the pancake is golden on the bottom and dry on top turn it on to a sheet of greaseproof paper.

14 Re-butter the pan with the pad of paper and continue cooking the pancakes until all the batter has been used.

15 To stuff the pancakes place one, cooked side upwards, on a board and spread a tablespoon of the filling over one half; turn in the sides and roll up the pancake into a long thin cigar shape.

16 Repeat the process until you have used all the pancakes and filling.

17 To serve, heat 50 g (2 oz) butter and 2 teaspoons of oil in a large frying pan and when it stops foaming place the blintzes in the pan, join side upwards.
18 Fry gently for about 3 minutes or until the underside is golden.
19 Turn and cook the other side until brown.
20 Serve plain or preferably with soured cream, or with honey or jam dribbled over the top.

Makes about 12

MATZO BLINTZES
Matzo pancakes

An alternative to the foregoing recipe is this Passover recipe, which is light and tasty.

> *Batter*
> 3 eggs, beaten
> 300 ml (½ pint) water
> 110 g (4 oz) matzo meal
> ½ teaspoon salt
> 50 g (2 oz) butter or margarine, melted

> *Filling:*
> 225 g (½ lb) cream cheese
> 1 egg, beaten
> 25 g (1 oz) sugar
> ½ teaspoon salt

> *For garnish:*
> Soured cream, honey or icing sugar

1 First prepare the filling by placing all the ingredients in a bowl and mixing until smooth. Set aside until required.

2 To make the batter, place the eggs, water, matzo meal and salt in a large bowl and mix well.

3 Heat a small 15–17.5 cm (6–7 in) frying pan and brush the base and sides with a little of the butter or margarine. Pour in enough batter to thinly coat the base of the pan and tilt it so that the batter spreads evenly. Cook until the bottom of the pancake is lightly browned and then slide it out onto a tea towel, cooked side up. Cook the remaining batter in the same way, lightly buttering the pan between each pancake.

4 Place 1 heaped tablespoon of the filling in the centre of each blintz and gently fold over the sides to form an envelope completely enclosing the filling. Take care not to crack the blintzes.

5 Heat the remaining butter in a large frying pan and fry each filled blintz on both sides until golden. Transfer to a serving plate and top with your chosen garnish.

Makes 8 blintzes (because of the matzo meal these pancakes will be thicker than in the previous recipe)

And finally, some good advice to all law-abiding Jews.
PESACH (Passover) – you can eat where you like, but not what you like.
SUCCOTH – You can eat what you like, but not where you like.
SHAVOUTH – You can eat whatever you like – wherever you like.

I would like to eat at a Maimouna with my Moroccan friends. Maimouna is a North African traditional way of celebrating the end of Passover. On the evening of the la.t day of the feast Muslim friends visited their Jewish neighbours to wish them happiness and prosperity. They arrived laden with food – honey, bread, fruit and vegetables; a fresh fish lavishly decorated (a symbol of fertility) which was cooked the following day in almonds. The following day the people went into the fields dressed in their traditional costumes, headdresses decorated with gold and silver coins, fingers and faces hennaed, dancing to the exhilarating rhythms of the music of the Meghreb.

In Morocco there would be camel and horse races and a great deal of shooting into the air. The entire field would be filled with the traditional noises of the 'You–You'. The air would be filled with good music, love, happiness, generosity and, above all, good food. For Moroccans are famed for their excellent food and the Jews have retained that tradition.

The celebration of Maimouna ('bring happiness' – in Arabic) is one tradition the Israeli Moroccans should not forget. For happiness comes too seldom, is too rare, and it must be enjoyed whenever possible.

On the feast of Maimouna, among many other dishes, the following frequently appear. I have given a recipe for Cous-cous, one for roasted red peppers, plus three different salads. These five dishes should feed 12–15 people.

COUS-COUS
North African beef stew

> Stew:
> 8 tablespoons oil
> 1 large onion, halved
> 900 g (2 lb) stewing beef, cut into large chunks
> 1 large tomato, halved
> 1 kohlrabi, halved

1 turnip, peeled and halved
3 sticks celery, halved
3 courgettes, halved
3 carrots, peeled and halved
2 tablespoons tomato purée
½ teaspoon chilli pepper
2 teaspoons salt
2 teaspoons cumin
½ cabbage, halved
3 potatoes, peeled
½ chicken, cut into pieces
225 g (8 oz) chickpeas, soaked overnight in cold water,
    drained and cooked in boiling water until tender

Cous-cous:
900 g (2 lb) cous-cous
50 g (2 oz) butter, chopped

1 The easiest way to prepare this dish is with a 'cous-cousier', but it is possible to use a steamer or a metal strainer that fits snugly over a large saucepan. Heat the oil in the base of the couscousier or steamer or in the saucepan and add all the stew ingredients except the potatoes, chicken and chickpeas. Fry for several minutes, stirring frequently. Add enough water to cover and bring to the boil. Lower the heat, cover the pan and simmer for about 2 hours or until the meat is tender.

2 Meanwhile pour the cous-cous onto a large baking sheet and sprinkle with warm, salted water. Work lightly between the fingers so that each grain is separate, moistened and beginning to swell. Leave to rest for 15 minutes. Repeat the process three times.

3 If using a couscousier place the cous-cous in the top.

Otherwise line the top of the steamer or the sieve with
a piece of fine muslin and then add the cous-cous.

4 When the meat in the stew is tender add the potatoes
and chicken pieces. Place the container containing the
cous-cous on top of the pan and cover. Continue to
simmer.

5 After 20 minutes stir the cous-cous with a fork, add the
pieces of butter, cover and continue to cook. After a
further 15–20 minutes stir the cous-cous to ensure the
even distribution of the butter.

6 To serve, pile the cous-cous into a serving dish.
Arrange the meat and chicken in the centre of a large
plate, lift the vegetables out of the stew with a slotted
spoon and arrange them around the meat. Add the
chickpeas to the stock, heat through and serve in a
separate bowl as a sauce.

FELFEL MEDGOUG
Roasted red peppers

8 large red peppers
6 tablespoons oil
Salt

1 Put the peppers on a baking tray and place in a
preheated oven, 200°C (400°F) Gas 6. Roast them for
about 20 minutes or until soft, turning frequently.

2 Remove the tray from the oven and, when the peppers
are cool enough to handle peel off the skin.

3 Cut the peppers in half and remove the seeds.

4 Heat the oil in a large frying pan and fry the peppers
until their colour darkens.

5 Sprinkle to taste with salt and serve hot or cold.

ZRODIYA CHALDA
Carrot salad

900 g (2 lb) carrots, peeled and grated
6 tablespoons finely chopped parsley
120 ml (4 fl oz) oil
4 tablespoons lemon juice or vinegar
3 cloves garlic, crushed
1½ teaspoons salt
½ teaspoon black pepper

1 Place the carrots and parsley in a large bowl and mix well.
2 Place the remaining ingredients in a small bowl and whisk with a fork. Pour over the carrots and toss well.

MARMOUNA
Spicy salad

3 tablespoons oil
2 courgettes, thinly sliced
3 cloves garlic, halved
2 chilli peppers, cut into strips
4 green peppers, thickly sliced
6 tomatoes, quartered
2 teaspoons salt
½ teaspoon powdered saffron dissolved in 2
   tablespoons hot water

1 Heat the oil in a pan and sauté the courgette slices until golden. Add all the remaining ingredients and enough water just to cover and bring to the boil. Lower the heat, cover the pan and cook for about 1 hour. Uncover and continue to simmer until the liquid has evaporated. Serve cold.

SALADE MUGHRABI
Aubergine salad

> 2 aubergines
> Juice of 1 lemon
> 2 tablespoons hot pepper sauce or ½ teaspoon chilli
>   pepper
> 1½ teaspoons salt
> 1 tablespoon oil

1 Place the aubergines in a large saucepan half filled with water and bring to the boil. Simmer until tender and then drain.
2 When cool enough to handle, peel and halve the aubergines then put them in a large bowl and mash with a fork.
3 Add the remaining ingredients and mix well.

Serves 4

Bibliography

Jewish Folklore, Nathan Ausubal, Valentine Mitchell, London 1948

The Jews, Chaim Bermant, Weidenfeld and Nicolson, London 1977

The Prophet Motive: Israel today and tomorrow, Georges Mikes, André Deutsch, London 1969

Everyday Life in Babylon and Assyria, Georges Contenau, Edward Arnold, London 1954

The Wisdom of Israel, Lewis Browne, Four Square, London 1962

The Complete American-Jewish Cookbook, A. London and B.K. Bishov, World Publishing, New York 1952

Treasury of Jewish Quotations, Leo Rostens, W.H. Allen, London and New York 1973

Anthology of Modern Hebrew Poetry, A. Birman, Abelard-Schuman, New York 1968

Fourteen Israeli Poets, ed. Dennis Silk, André Deutsch, London 1976

The Golden Peacock – Yiddish Poetry, ed. Joseph Leftnich, Sci-art Publishers, Cambridge, Mass. 1939

Die Schönsten lieder der Ostjuden, F.M. Kaufmann, Judischer Varlog, Berlin 1920

Israel, Uri Davis, Zed Press, London 1977

In King David's Footsteps, Hans Habe, W.H. Allen, London 1973

The Walled Garden, Chaim Bermant, Weidenfeld and Nicolson, London 1974

Pomegranate Tree in Jerusalem, Lerubavel Gilead, Translated D. Krook, Hakibbutz Hameuchad Publishing House, Tel-Aviv 1983

Index